DEATH AND RESURRECTION

DEATH AND RESURRECTION

MEDITATIONS ON HOLY WEEK FROM THE CHURCH FATHERS

by
VINCENT A. YZERMANS

with Scripture Readings
from the Revised Standard Version

Foreword by
Most Reverend Peter W. Bartholome, D.D.,
Bishop of St. Cloud

THE LITURGICAL PRESS

ST. JOHN'S ABBEY   COLLEGEVILLE, MINNESOTA

The excerpts from the Revised Standard Version of the Bible are used with the express permission of the Division of Christian Education of the National Council of the Churches of Christ in the United States of America, owner of the copyright.

Photographs of sixth-century mosaics from the Church of St. Apollinaris, Ravenna, courtesy of Stabilimento D. Anderson, Rome.

Nihil obstat: John Eidenschink, O.S.B., J.C.D., *Censor deputatus. Imprimatur*: ✠ Peter W. Bartholome, D.D., Bishop of St. Cloud. February 18, 1963.

Copyright 1963 by The Order of St. Benedict, Inc., Collegeville, Minnesota.

Printed in the U.S.A. by the Sentinel Publishing Co., St. Cloud, Minnesota.

To my
brother and sisters
Louis
Mary
Joan
Rose Marie

FOREWORD

"Spiritual reading," wrote St. Bernard of Clairvaux, "is the oil of the lamp of prayer." At no time in the Church's year does the lamp of prayer need refueling as much as during the great days of Holy Week. This modest work, authored by a priest of our Diocese of Saint Cloud, is the oil for our lamps of prayer during these great days of our salvation.

All the things that the great spiritual writers have to say about the importance and necessity of spiritual reading apply *par excellence* to the reading of God's own words, the Holy Bible. To read *about* the passion, death and resurrection of the Blessed Savior is salutary, without a doubt. However, to read the passion, death and resurrection of Christ according to the inspired account of the four evangelists is infinitely superior.

A major part of this book is the chronological narration of these great events which brought the Savior's life to a glorious triumph in tragedy and majesty as He walked among us on this earth. For this very reason Pope John XXIII recently urged the faithful to read the Holy Bible, from which, he said, "is to be drawn not only deep moral teaching, but also a more vital understanding of Christianity and of the redeeming work of Christ."

The other half of this book is a series of meditations based on the actual words of many Fathers of the Church. These quotations, skillfully woven together to form a spiritual mosaic, will afford the reader many hours of quiet meditation. In our age of so many distracting noises this type of quietude is as much a necessity for the body as it always is for the soul. The careful reading of these meditations will present insights into the passion, death and resurrection of Christ that often times are forgotten in our too-busy world.

The sacred liturgy of these great days is so rich and its mood changes so rapidly from day to day, and even within the course of the same day, that all of us will find that private spiritual reading and meditation will inevitably give us a deeper appreciation and understanding of these liturgical, community actions. By enriching our own souls individually we will thereby be able to share more fully with the community the graces the Savior pours into our hearts and minds through serious spiritual reading.

It is my ardent wish, therefore, that this modest book will be a means to help the individual participate more fully in the spirit of Holy Week and by so doing find his proper relationship to the Christian community. Spiritual reading of this kind will undoubtedly enkindle the spirit of prayer which must always be the foundation of sincere Christian thinking and living.

✠ PETER W. BARTHOLOME
Bishop of Saint Cloud

Ash Wednesday
February 27, 1963

TABLE OF CONTENTS

DEATH AND RESURRECTION

PALM SUNDAY

The sacred drama of Holy Week begins with a shout of praise: "Blessed is He who comes in the name of the Lord!" Today, too, children raise the cry: "Hosanna in the highest!" This is the day of triumph. Christ rides into the holy city Jerusalem and is hailed as King.

This is the week of triumph. Christ lives in the holy city which is His Church, and His people joyfully acclaim Him King. The holy bishop Methodius cries out for all of us:

> Blessed is He who comes in the name of the Lord, for He is the Lord who will have mercy upon the creatures of His hands.... Blessed is He who comes in the name of the Lord, for He is the Lord who will save all men who have been lost in error by putting away all error and sending light to those who are lost in darkness.... Blessed is He who comes in the name of the Lord, for He is the one who will give Himself for all of us. He will deliver the poor from the hands of their oppressors. He will pour wine and oil upon him who had fallen among thieves and had been overlooked by so many.... Blessed is He who comes in the name of the Lord for He is the Lord who will save us by Himself. No ambassador, no angel, but the Lord Himself will save us.

The triumphal entry of the holy One sets the theme for our hymn of praise and adoration this week. We become a part of the throng who welcome the Savior every Palm Sunday; we go forth with joy to meet Him, inviting Him to come into the holy city of our souls. We take to heart the advice of Methodius:

> Let us, with the children, raise our branches on high and with them make a joyous applause so that the Holy Spirit will breathe also upon us and enable us in our own way to cry out the hymn taught by God Himself, "Blessed is He who comes in the name of the Lord".... Today the King of glory is praised throughout the world and invites us to be partakers of His heavenly banquet. In this way He shows that He is the Lord of both heaven and earth, just as both those in heaven and upon earth now glorify Him with the same hymn of praise.

PALM SUNDAY

The Messiah's triumphal entry into Jerusalem

MATTHEW 21:1-5

And when they drew near to Jerusalem and came to Bethphage, to the Mount of Olives, then Jesus sent two disciples, saying to them, "Go into the village opposite you, and immediately you will find an ass tied, and a colt with her; untie them and bring them to me. If any one says anything to you, you shall say, 'The Lord has need of them,' and he will send them immediately." This took place to fulfil what was spoken by the prophet, saying,
"Tell the daughter of Zion,
Behold, your king is coming to you,
humble, and mounted on an ass,
and on a colt, the foal of an ass."

LUKE 19:32-44

So those who were sent went away and found it as he had told them. And as they were untying the colt, its owners said to them, "Why are you untying the colt?" And they said, "The Lord has need of it." And they brought it to Jesus, and throwing their garments on the colt they set Jesus upon it. And as he rode along, they spread their garments on the road. As he was now drawing near, at the descent of the Mount of Olives, the whole multitude of the disciples began to rejoice and praise God with a loud voice for all the mighty works that they had seen, saying, "Blessed be the King who comes in the name of the Lord! Peace in

With this spirit, Holy Week will have a deeper meaning for all of us. It will be infinitely more than a rigorous spiritual marathon. Rather, it will be the time of our renewal, the time of joyous praise, the time of loving and grateful union with Christ who is our love and joy. This was the week for which the Son of God was born; this is the week for which each Christian is born.

We were created to share in the suffering and death and, at the very same time, in the glory and resurrection of our Savior. The response we give the Savior in His agony is the measure of our sharing in His glory. Thus Saint Augustine admonishes us today with the words he addressed to his flock in northern Africa centuries ago:

> Although Christians should be conspicuous in every season of the year by their prayers, fasts, and alms-deeds, this season especially should arouse even those who are indifferent at other times. Even those who are conscientious in performing these works at other times should now perform them with even greater diligence. These days, when the sufferings of the Lord Christ are renewed, should remind us that our life in this world is a time for continually practicing humility.

That humility which is the cornerstone of the Christian life is the necessary condition for fruitful participation in the events of this great week. Setting before us the example of Christ's humility, the Bishop of Hippo continues:

> What mercy could be greater, so far as we poor sinners are concerned, than that which drew the Creator of the heavens down from heaven, clothed the maker of the earth with earthly garments, made Him, who in eternity remains equal to His Father, equal to us in mortality, and imposed on the Lord of the universe the form of a servant? He who is our food hungers; He who is our fulfillment thirsts; He who is our strength becomes weak; He who is our health suffers; He who is our life dies.

We shall not be able to enter into the spirit of these sacred days unless we have a humble and contrite heart. Without humility, we cannot begin to comprehend the meaning that pierces every moment of these days. Saint John Chrysostom gives us this counsel:

> Think of who He is who is so close to you in this tremendous sacrifice and with whom you are invited to call upon God.... This will help you to be recollected in spirit when you reflect that, in spite of being enclosed in a body and clothed with flesh, you have been deemed worthy to praise the Lord of all with the citizens of heaven. Do not, then, take part in this holy praise, in these sacred mysteries, with a dissipated soul. Let not your thoughts during these days be occupied with worldly matters. Rather, casting all earthly things from your mind... offer your holy praise to God for all that He has done for you.

Without humility we cannot worthily offer God that praise which is His due. Each of us must be so thoroughly convinced of our need for humility that we are constantly conscious of it. This conviction is born only after serious reflection and meditation. Holy Week is the time for us to begin or to continue this serious meditation. During these days we should abstain from worldly interests just as rigorously as we abstain from heaven and glory in the highest!" And some of the Pharisees in the multitude said to him, "Teacher, rebuke your disciples." He answered, "I tell you, if these were silent, the very stones would cry out."

And when he drew near and saw the city he wept over it, saying, "Would that even today you knew the things that make for peace! But now they are hid from your eyes. For the days shall come upon you, when your enemies will cast up a bank about you and surround you, and hem you in on every side, and dash you to the ground, you and your children within you, and they will not leave one stone upon another in you; because you did not know the time of your visitation."

MATTHEW 21:10-16

And when he entered Jerusalem, all the city was stirred, saying, "Who is this?" And the crowds said, "This is the prophet Jesus from Nazareth of Galilee."

And Jesus entered the temple of God and drove out all who sold and bought in the temple, and he overturned the tables of the money-changers and the seats of those who sold pigeons. He said to them, "It is written, 'My house shall be called a house of prayer'; but you make it a den of robbers."

And the blind and the lame came to him in the temple, and he healed them. But when the chief priests and the scribes saw the wonderful things that he did, and the children crying out in the temple, "Hosanna to the Son of David!" they were indignant; and they said to him, "Do you hear what these are saying?" And Jesus said to them, "Yes; have you never read,

'Out of the mouth of babes and sucklings
thou hast brought perfect praise'?"

Christ's last words to the people

JOHN 12:20-36

Now among those who went up to worship at the feast were some Greeks. So these came to Philip, who was from Beth-saida in Galilee, and said to him, "Sir, we wish to see Jesus." Philip went and told Andrew; Andrew went with Philip and they told Jesus. And Jesus answered them, "The hour has come for the Son of man to be glorified. Truly, truly, I say to you, unless a grain of wheat falls into the earth and dies, it remains alone; but if it worldly pleasures. This is the type of fasting Saint John Chrysostom enjoins when he says:

> When you were fasting I used to say to you that there could be one of you who, while fasting, was not fasting. So now I say that it is possible that a person can fast by not fasting. Perhaps you think I am speaking in riddles, so I shall explain. How can it be that a person who is fasting does not fast? When a person abstains from food but not from sin. How can it be that a person who is not fasting still fasts? When he partakes of food but abstains from sin. This latter fast is better than the former — not only better but also easier.

Through such fasting, both from sin and from the enticements of the world's distractions, we shall find time for quiet meditation. Foregoing unnecessary involvement in daily living will give us leisure — leisure, as Saint Augustine says, "not for indulging in pleasure but for searching after wisdom." Quoting Holy Scripture, he continues: "The wisdom of the scribe comes in leisure time and he who abstains from unnecessary business shall receive wisdom. In this way the mind has time for thoughts of God."

The Christian should strive after this quiet meditation every possible moment during this great week. The subject of his meditation is given by holy mother Church, thoughts that recur day after day, beginning as an imperceptible cloud during the triumphal entry into Jerusalem until it rumbles in the heavy overcast on Good Friday and is finally dissipated by the glorious rays of the rising Son on Easter morning. The theme is the text of Saint Paul: "And being found in human form He humbled Himself and became obedient unto death, even death on a cross. Therefore God also has exalted Him and has bestowed upon Him the name that is above every name, so that at the name of Jesus every knee should bend of those in heaven, on earth and under the earth, and every tongue should confess that the Lord Jesus Christ is in the glory of God the Father" (Phil. 2:8-11).

Our reflection on this central idea of Christianity will form the solid foundation for our humility. From the shame of the cross to the glory of the resurrection, we learn the path that each of us must follow in our journey to everlasting glory. In His footsteps we shall find our sure footing. His actions become our examples, as Saint Hilary of Poitiers saw so clearly:

> Christ prayed for His persecutors because they knew not what they did. He promised paradise from the cross, because He is God the King. He rejoiced upon the cross, that all was finished when He drank the vinegar, because He had fulfilled all the prophecies before He died. He was born for us, suffered for us, died for us, rose again for us.

Christ is our model. We must follow Him. His purpose must be our purpose. The Venerable Bede explains that divine purpose in these words:

> The whole divine mission of our Redeemer in the flesh was to restore peace to the world. For this reason He became man, suffered and rose from the dead. In such a way He brought back to the peace of God those who by offending God had incurred His anger.... The Apostle, writing about Him to those converted from paganism, says, "And He

dies, it bears much fruit. He who loves his life loses it, and he who hates his life in this world will keep it for eternal life. If any one serves me, he must follow me; and where I am, there shall my servant be also; if any one serves me, the Father will honor him.

"Now is my soul troubled. And what shall I say, 'Father, save me from this hour'? No, for this purpose I have come to this hour. Father, glorify thy name." Then a voice came from heaven, "I have glorified it, and I will glorify it again." The crowd standing by heard it and said that it had thundered. Others said, "An angel has spoken to him." Jesus answered, "This voice has come for your sake, not for mine. Now is the judgment of this world, now shall the ruler of this world be cast out; and I, when I am lifted up from the earth, will draw all men to myself." He said this to show by what death he was to die. The crowd answered him, "We have heard from the law that the Christ remains for ever. How can you say that the Son of man must be lifted up? Who is this Son of man?" Jesus said to them, "The light is with you for a little longer. Walk while you have the light, lest the darkness overtake you; he who walks in the darkness does not know where he goes. While you have the light, believe in the light, that you may become sons of light."

When Jesus had said this, he departed and hid himself from them.

He retires to Bethany for the night

MATTHEW 21:17

And leaving them, he went out of the city to Bethany and lodged there.

MONDAY IN HOLY WEEK

Jesus curses a fig tree

MARK 11:12-14

On the following day, when they came from Bethany, he was hungry. And seeing in the distance a fig tree in leaf, he went to see if he could find

came and preached peace to you who were far off and peace to those who were near; for through Him we both have access in one Spirit to the Father" (Eph. 2:17-18).

Saint Methodius expresses the same thought:

> The Lamb and Son of God did all these things ... so that, on our behalf, He might undergo His saving passion and be recognized, as it were, in the market-place. In such a way those who bought Him for thirty pieces of silver might recognize Him who, with His life-giving Blood, was to redeem the world. Christ, our Passover, was sacrificed for us in order that those who were sprinkled with His precious blood ... might escape from the darts of the destroyer.

It is not good, however, to exaggerate in our meditations on the Savior's passion and death. They are only part of the drama of our redemption. Overemphasis on the Lord's passion and death would produce a Christianity of doom; even the youngest child knows that Christianity is a life of joy. We were made for happiness. Thus an integral part of Holy Week, the third dimension of Christian living, lives in resurrection. We shall be reminded of this thought continually during these solemn days. Death to sin is the threshold of life in Christ. Good Friday is the condition of Easter. Even among the first readings on Good Friday, when we are rightly saddened by the Savior's death, Mother Church strikes a note of joy: "The third day He shall rise again." With this thought in mind Saint Augustine observed:

> The prophet says, "We have seen Him." What is He like? "He had no form or comeliness." Why is this? asks another prophet. "I can count all My bones." They have numbered His bones as He hung upon the cross. An ugly sight — the sight of one crucified. But that ugliness produced beauty. What beauty? That of the resurrection, because He is "beautiful above all the sons of men."

Holy Week would be folly if the resurrection were not an essential part of it. It is true that we shall climb to the summit of Calvary and stand beneath the cross of Christ, but we never forget that Calvary is the entrance to the valley of the resurrection. Thus Saint Augustine admonishes us:

> Since our Lord Jesus Christ made one day dolorous by His death and another glorious by His resurrection, let us, by recalling both days in solemn commemoration, keep sacred the memory of His death and rejoice in the celebration of His resurrection. This is our annual festival. It is our Passover, not symbolized by the slaying of an animal as in the case of the ancient people, but fulfilled by the Victim of salvation for a new people. ... In our grief over His death and our joy in His **resurrection we are happy** because He endured sorrow and anticipated joy for our sake. We do not live in ungrateful forgetfulness but we celebrate in grateful memory.

The same saint elsewhere says: "If we unhesitatingly believe with the heart what we profess with the mouth, in Christ we are crucified, we are dead, we are buried. And with Christ we are raised from the dead on the third day."

anything on it. When he came to it, he found nothing but leaves, for it was not the season for figs. And he said to it, "May no one ever eat fruit from you again." And his disciples heard it.

Jesus cleanses the temple a second time

MARK 11:15-18

And they came to Jerusalem. And he entered the temple and began to drive out those who sold and those who bought in the temple, and he overturned the tables of the money-changers and the seats of those who sold pigeons; and he would not allow any one to carry anything through the temple. And he taught, and said to them, "Is it not written, 'My house shall be called a house of prayer for all the nations'? But you have made it a den of robbers." And the chief priests and the scribes heard it and sought a way to destroy him; for they feared him, because all the multitude was astonished at his teaching.

Return to Bethany

MARK 11:19

And when evening came they went out of the city.

TUESDAY IN HOLY WEEK

The withered fig tree

MARK 11:20-26

As they passed by in the morning, they saw the fig tree withered away to its roots. And Peter remembered and said to him, "Master, look! The fig tree which you cursed has withered." And Jesus answered them, "Have faith in God. Truly, I say to you, whoever says to this mountain, 'Be taken up and cast into the sea,' and does not doubt in his heart, but believes that what he says will come to pass, it will be done for him. Therefore I tell you, whatever you ask in prayer, believe that you receive it, and you will. And whenever you stand praying, forgive, if you have anything against any one; so that your Father also who is in heaven may forgive you your trespasses. But if you do not forgive,

Christ was the first to experience this leap from death to resurrection, from ugliness to beauty from sorrow to joy. Every Christian shares the same experience at baptism. Our thoughts return lovingly and gratefully to that great day when each of us died and rose again in Christ through the life-giving water of baptism. More than any other event in our lives, baptism should make us mindful of this intimate union of death and resurrection. Considered in such a way, Holy Week is neither a tragedy nor a contest. It is our annual renunciation of sin, our annual foretaste of glory. For this reason we enter into the spirit of these days with the "grateful memory" Saint Augustine requested. This same thought was expressed by Saint John Damascene:

> Through His birth, that is His incarnation, and baptism and passion and resurrection, He delivered our nature from the sin of our first parents and death and corruption. He became the first-fruits of the resurrection and made Himself the way and image and pattern in order that we, too, following in His footsteps, may become by adoption what He is Himself by nature, sons and heirs of God and joint heirs with Him . . . . He gave us, therefore, a second birth in order that, just as we who are born of Adam are in his image and are the heirs of the curse and corruption, so also being born of Christ we may be in His likeness and heirs of His incorruption and glory.

The Venerable Bede draws the parallel between death and resurrection even more strikingly:

> In what way could men be more truly encouraged to believe in the glory to come and to strive for eternal life than by knowing that God Himself had become a sharer of their humanity and mortality? In what other way could they be asked more effectively to suffer evils of every kind for the sake of salvation than by learning that their own Creator had suffered at the hands of wicked men every kind of abuse and even the sentence of death itself? For what reason could they more certainly accept the hope of resurrection than through remembering that they had been cleansed and sanctified by His sacraments and made one in His body who, tasting death for their sake, hastened to become the exemplar of their resurrection?

The first conviction we gain from Holy Week should be a deeper appreciation of the inseparable unity of our Savior's death and resurrection. This conviction will enrich our meditations on the great liturgical events of the week; it will also afford our meditations on the need for humility a deeper well from which to draw reasons and examples. Our meditations are the condition, the Savior's death and resurrection the subject, and a God-given humility the result.

During these days we shall be spiritual beggars. Prelate or priest, religious or layman, old or young, rich or poor, not one of us can afford not to beg for the graces our merciful Savior wishes to share with us these days. Saint or sinner, wise or foolish, strong or weak, not one of us can excuse himself from the spiritual exercises of this week, for as Saint John Chrysostom remarked:

neither will your Father who is in heaven forgive your trespasses."

The authority of Jesus

MATTHEW 21:23-27

And when he entered the temple, the chief priests and the elders of the people came up to him as he was teaching, and said, "By what authority are you doing these things, and who gave you this authority?" Jesus answered them, "I also will ask you a question; and if you tell me the answer, then I also will tell you by what authority I do these things. The baptism of John, whence was it? From heaven or from men?" And they argued with one another, "If we say, 'From heaven,' he will say to us, 'Why then did you not believe him?' But if we say, 'From men,' we are afraid of the multitude; for all hold that John was a prophet." So they answered Jesus, "We do not know." And he said to them, "Neither will I tell you by what authority I do these things."

WEDNESDAY IN HOLY WEEK

The council and the betrayal

MATTHEW 26:1-5,14-16

When Jesus had finished all these sayings, he said to his disciples, "You know that after two days the Passover is coming, and the Son of man will be delivered up to be crucified."

Then the chief priests and the elders of the people gathered in the palace of the high priest, who was called Caiaphas, and took counsel together in order to arrest Jesus by stealth and kill him. But they said, "Not during the feast, lest there be a tumult among the people."

Then one of the twelve, who was called Judas Iscariot, went to the chief priests and said, "What will you give me if I deliver him to you?" And they paid him thirty pieces of silver. And from that moment he sought an opportunity to betray him.

Just as soil left uncultivated by the farmer goes wild and becomes un-
lovely, so likewise the soul that goes without spiritual cultivation brings
forth weeds and thistles.   If those who each day hear the teaching of the
prophets and apostles and sing from their hearts the songs of Holy
Scripture have difficulty in containing their own fiery hearts, checking
their anger, freeing themselves from the poison of envy, mastering their
own concupiscence, restraining all these wild beasts — what hope of salvation have they who never use these saving medicines or never listen to
the divine teaching?   Just as he who abandons a refuge will stray in every
direction and he who goes without a light into the darkness will stumble
over many things, so he who forgets the fear of God will continually be
tormented by cares and pains and anxieties.

Has not each of us experienced these "anxieties"? Do we not need these
sacred days to rediscover the fundamentals of Christian life and thought?

The closer our union with Christ through the liturgy of the Church, the
greater will be our spiritual gifts from Christ through the saving prayers of
His Church.   Thus Saint John Chrysostom insisted that his people take their
place in their parish churches and actively participate in the ceremonies of
these days.   He countenanced no excuse:

I would like to know what they are doing who neglect the assemblies of
the faithful and keep away from this sacred table.   I know only too well.
They are either talking about vain or idle things or immersed in worldly
things.   In either case the time used is without justification and merits
severe correction.   There is no need to prove the negligence of the first
group.   Nor can they be excused who offer the excuse of family duties
and of the needs that arise from them.   It is obvious that they do not
value spiritual and heavenly things above those of this world.   What
servant, I ask you, attends to the things of his own house before fulfilling
those of his master?

Rather than be numbered among those who keep this great week in "ungrate-
ful forgetfulness," we should earnestly strive to "celebrate in grateful memory"
the mysteries of our Savior's passion, death, and resurrection by participating
in the sacred rites performed in our parish church.   We should take to heart
the admonition of Saint Leo the Great:

Let us glorify God in our body so that we may show that He is dwelling
in us by the holiness of our lives.   Since no virtues are more worthy or
more excellent than merciful loving-kindness and unblemished chastity,
let us especially gird ourselves with these weapons.   Thus raised from the
earth, as it were, on the two wings of active charity and shining purity,
we may secure for ourselves a place in heaven.

This is the purpose of our meditations these days. Holy Week points
heavenward. The more ardently we enter into the spirit of this week, the
more certain we shall be of entering into the glory of heaven. Saint Ambrose
summarizes what our sentiments should be:

With me and for me He suffers. For me He is sad. For me He is
burned. In my stead, therefore, and in my place He grieved who had
no reason to grieve for Himself. Not Thy wounds, but mine, hurt Thee,
Lord Jesus. . . . Just as Thy death made an end of death and Thy wounds
healed our scars, so also Thy sorrow took away our sorrow.

Judas betrays Jesus with a kiss.

HOLY THURSDAY

How can we give expression to a day so full of meaning? Christ is the central figure. Two others, Peter and Judas, play minor roles.

The day begins in the early hours. We might find ourselves among the privileged few who take part in the morning Mass of the Chrism. The bishop gathers his priests and people about himself in the cathedral church to consecrate the sacred oils to be used in every church throughout the coming year. Gathered together in worship and service, bishop and priests recall the Lord and His apostles in the upper room. Together they worship God in the name of God's people. Together they are bound in a ministry of service, for the holy oils consecrated this morning will be used for the salvation of God's chosen people. Perhaps no utterance is given; but each, from the bishop to the youngest priest, hears again in his own heart the Master's description of His priesthood which His ministers have chosen as their way of life: "The Son of man came not to be served but to serve, and to give His life as a ransom for many" (Matthew 20:28).

These holy oils that they have come together to consecrate remind each of God's ministers of his vocation as the servant of the servants of God. Through the use of the holy oils both bishop and priests will carry out the work of the Master. Thus no pains must be spared to make this Mass of the Chrism the most solemn and sacred. Priests from far and near make every effort to take their station and exercise their ministry together with their bishop who consecrates the holy oils. No ceremony of the year can compare with the richness of this rite.

This is as it should be, for, as Saint Cyril of Jerusalem remarked, "this exorcised oil receives such power by the prayer of the bishop that it not only burns and cleanses away the traces of sin but also chases away all the invisible powers of the evil one." Guided by the vision of faith, the worshipper should look upon the holy oil and the sacred chrism as the life-giving and life-sustaining spiritual signs that they really are. Thus the same patriarch of Jerusalem admonished his flock:

HOLY THURSDAY

Preparation for the Passover

LUKE 22:7-13

Then came the day of Unleavened Bread, on which the passover lamb had to be sacrificed. So Jesus sent Peter and John saying, "Go and prepare the passover for us, that we may eat it." They said to him, "Where will you have us prepare it?" He said to them, "Behold, when you have entered the city, a man carrying a jar of water will meet you; follow him into the house which he enters, and tell the householder, 'The Teacher says to you, Where is the guest room, where I am to eat the passover with my disciples?' And he will show you a large upper room furnished; there make ready." And they went, and found it as he had told them; and they prepared the passover.

The Last Supper

LUKE 22:14-18

And when the hour came, he sat at table, and the apostles with him. And he said to them, "I have earnestly desired to eat this passover with you before I suffer; for I tell you I shall not eat it until it is fulfilled in the kingdom of God." And he took a cup, and when he had given thanks he said, "Take this, and divide it among yourselves; for I tell you that from now on I shall not drink of the fruit of the vine until the kingdom of God comes."

> Beware of supposing this to be ordinary ointment. This holy ointment is . . . after the invocation the gift of Christ, and by the presence of His Godhead it brings to us the Holy Spirit. It is, accordingly, applied to the forehead and the other senses so that while the body is anointed with visible ointment, the soul is made holy by the holy and life-giving Spirit.

Every Catholic owes it to himself to participate at least once in his life in the Mass of the Chrism. At no other time in his life and in no other place will he ever share in a rite so rich in meaning. In his cathedral church, the mother of all churches in a diocese, the Catholic will discover by his own participation in these sacred rites the unity of faith that binds together the bishop, priests, and people of a diocese.

Holy Thursday is also the anniversary of the priesthood. Christ is at all times the eternal High Priest, for on this day above all others He performed his high-priestly tasks. Thus Saint Ambrose says:

> It is a priest's duty to offer something and, according to the Law, to enter into the holy places by means of blood. Seeing, then, that God had rejected the blood of bulls and goats, Christ the High Priest was indeed bound to make passage and entry into the Holy of Holies of heaven through His own Blood, in order that He might be the everlasting satisfaction for our sins.

Every priest shares in this priesthood of Christ — not for himself but for others. This day he renews his dedication by professing before the heavenly court that he, too, is willing and ready to shed his blood if necessary for his people.

Holy Thursday is the day of love, of thanksgiving, the day of God's giving of Himself in the Holy Eucharist. As we are gathered in our parish churches, we do not settle for the quick, on-the-go, almost makeshift Mass and Communion at the end of a tiring day at the office or shop; rather, we gather with our fellow members of Christ in the great, solemn liturgical evening rites. Then we are rested. Then we have time for contemplation and meditation. We come together in the evening to find ourselves, to find our real identity as members of the parish, the localized Mystical Body of Christ. This is a community feast. This night we find our unity in Christ, both in the Holy Eucharist and in the example He leaves us in the washing of the feet.

Imagine, for a moment, what this world would be like without the sacramental presence of Christ. Imagine what we would be like without the sustaining strength of Holy Communion. This is the night of our thanksgiving.

Nothing so radically uproots our selfishness as the community that was born when Christ first took bread and wine and made them the life-bearing signs of His own Body and Blood. That great sacramentalist, Saint Cyril of Jerusalem, explains the meaning of this action in these words:

> He once turned water into wine in Cana of Galilee at His own will. Is it incredible that He should have turned wine into Blood? When called to an earthly marriage He miraculously performed that wonderful work.

The quarrel over precedence

LUKE 22:24-30

A dispute also arose among them, which of them was to be regarded as the greatest. And he said to them, "The kings of the Gentiles exercise lordship over them; and those in authority over them are called benefactors. But not so with you; rather let the greatest among you become as the youngest and the leader as one who serves. For which is the greater, one who sits at table, or one who serves? Is it not the one who sits at table? But I am among you as one who serves.

"You are those who have continued with me in my trials; as my Father appointed a kingdom for me, so do I appoint for you that you may eat and drink at my table in my kingdom, and sit on thrones judging the twelve tribes of Israel."

Jesus washes His disciples' feet

JOHN 13:1-20

Now before the feast of the Passover, when Jesus knew that his hour had come to depart out of this world to the Father, having loved his own who were in the world, he loved them to the end. And during supper, when the devil had already put it into the heart of Judas Iscariot, Simon's son, to betray him, Jesus, knowing that the Father had given all things into his hands, and that he had come from God and was going to God, rose from supper, laid aside his garments, and girded himself with a towel. Then he poured water into a basin, and began to wash the disciples' feet, and to wipe them with the towel with which he was girded. He came to Simon Peter; and Peter said to him, "Lord, do you wash my feet?" Jesus answered him, "What I am doing you do not know now, but afterward you will understand." Peter said to him, "You shall never wash my feet." Jesus answered him, "If I do not wash you, you have no part in me." Simon Peter said to him, "Lord, not my feet only but also my hands and my head!" Jesus said to him, "He who has bathed does not need to wash, except for his feet, but he is clean all over; and you are clean, but not all of you." For he knew who was to betray him; that was why he said, "You are not all clean."

When he had washed their feet, and taken his garments, and resumed his place, he said to them,

Should He not also eagerly bestow His Body and Blood on the children of the bridal chamber? Therefore, with certain faith let us partake of the Body and Blood of Christ.... In such a way we come to bear Christ in us, because His Body and Blood are diffused through our members. Thus it is that, according to the blessed Peter, "we become partakers of the divine nature" (2 Peter 1:4).

We are one in God. We share the same divinity. There can be no room for selfish individualism in the life of the true Christian. The closer we approach Christ, the closer we approach each other. "When you mention Communion," says Saint John Damascene, "it is an actual coming together, because through it we have communion with Christ and share in His flesh and His divinity. Indeed, we also have communion and are united with one another through it. Since we partake of one bread, we all become the one Body and Blood of Christ and members of one another, being of one body with Christ." The Christian is his brother's keeper. For that reason we pray for all men in the celebration of the Eucharist, just as Christ Himself prayed for all men at the first eucharistic service. Saint Cyril of Jerusalem summarizes the Christian's prayer:

After the spiritual sacrifice is perfected...we entreat God for the common peace of the Church, for the tranquility of the world, for kings, for soldiers and allies, for the sick, for the afflicted. In a word, for all who stand in need of help we all pray and offer this Sacrifice.... When we offer to Him our supplications for those who have died, though they be sinners, we offer up Christ, sacrificed for our sins, propitiating our merciful God both for them and for ourselves.

The whole wide world, with all its trouble and turmoil, conflict and crisis, is the personal concern of the sincere Christian. His embracing love enfolds all races, all peoples, and "especially those of the household of the faith" (Gal. 6:10). This night, then, we renew our faith in the most wondrous of all God's gifts. With firm conviction we acknowledge the words of Saint John Damascene:

The bread and wine are not merely figures of the Body and Blood of Christ (God forbid!) but the deified Body of the Lord Himself, for the Lord has said, "This is My Body," not a figure of My Body; and "My Blood," not a figure of My Blood.

Confirming our faith, Saint Ambrose reminds us:

The sacrament which you receive is made what it is by the word of Christ.... You read concerning the making of the whole world: "He spoke, and it came to be; He commanded, and it stood forth." Shall not the word of Christ, which was able to make out of nothing that which was not, be able to change things which already exist into what they were not? The Lord Jesus Himself proclaims: "This is My Body." Before the blessing of the heavenly words another nature is spoken of. After the consecration the Body is signified.... And you say, "Amen," that is, "It is true." Let the heart within confess what the mouth utters. Let the soul feel what the voice speaks. Christ, then, feeds His Church with this sacrament and by means of it the life of the soul is strengthened.

"Do you know what I have done to you? You call me Teacher and Lord; and you are right, for so I am. If I then, your Lord and Teacher, have washed your feet, you also ought to wash one another's feet. For I have given you an example, that you also should do as I have done to you. Truly, truly, I say to you, a servant is not greater than his master; nor is he who is sent greater than he who sent him. If you know these things, blessed are you if you do them. I am not speaking of you all; I know whom I have chosen; it is that the scripture may be fulfilled, 'He who ate my bread has lifted his heel against me.' I tell you this now, before it takes place, that when it does take place you may believe that I am he. Truly, truly, I say to you, he who receives any one whom I send receives me; and he who receives me receives him who sent me."

The betrayer

JOHN 13:21-30

When Jesus had thus spoken, he was troubled in spirit, and testified, "Truly, truly, I say to you, one of you will betray me." The disciples looked at one another, uncertain of whom he spoke. One of his disciples, whom Jesus loved, was lying close to the breast of Jesus; so Simon Peter beckoned to him and said, "Tell us who it is of whom he speaks." So lying thus, close to the breast of Jesus, he said to him, "Lord, who is it?" Jesus answered, "It is he to whom I shall give this morsel when I have dipped it." So when he had dipped the morsel, he gave it to Judas, the son of Simon Iscariot. Then after the morsel, Satan entered into him. Jesus said to him, "What you are going to do, do quickly." Now no one at the table knew why he said this to him. Some thought that, because Judas had the money box, Jesus was telling him, "Buy what we need for the feast"; or, that he should give something to the poor. So after receiving the morsel, he immediately went out; and it was night.

Institution of the Eucharist and the priesthood

1 COR. 11:23-25

For I received from the Lord what I also delivered to you, that the Lord Jesus on the night when he was betrayed took bread, and when he had given thanks, he broke it, and said, "This is my body which is for you. Do this in remembrance of me."

Without faith we are impoverished, for the mind cannot comprehend the brilliance nor the heart feel the warmth that surrounds the table of the Last Supper. If our faith asks why bread and wine were chosen as the signs of Christ's Body and Blood, Saint John Damascene answers:

> Bread and wine are employed because God knows man's weakness. For, in general, man turns away discontentedly from what is not well-worn by custom. So with His usual indulgence God performs His supernatural works through familiar objects. Take, for example, baptism. Man usually washes himself with water and anoints himself with oil. So God connected the grace of the Spirit with the oil, and the water He made the laver of re-birth. In a similar manner it is man's custom to eat and drink bread and wine. Thus God joined His divinity to these and made them His Body and Blood in order that we may rise to what is supernatural through what is familiar and natural.

Saint Ambrose presents another image for our consideration. He sees the Savior hanging on the cross as an image of the precious Blood of Christ in the Holy Eucharist:

> Here is the cup you use to purify the hidden recesses of your soul. It is not a cup of the Old Testament, filled with ordinary wine but a new cup, brought down from heaven to earth, filled with wine pressed from that wondrous cluster who hung in the flesh upon the tree of the cross just as grapes hang on the vine. From this sacred cluster, then, is the wine that makes the heart of man glad, uplifts the sorrowful, and pours into us the supreme joys of faith, true devotion, and purity.

Let us go to the words of Saint John Chrysostom in order to apply to ourselves all that we have been saying about the Holy Eucharist. The lesson is obvious: as Christians we can do nothing better than foster our union with Christ in Holy Communion. Saint John Chrysostom says:

> Let no poor person grieve because of his poverty, for this is the festival of the soul. Let no rich person take pride in his abundance, for money cannot add to the joy of this day.... The same table is prepared both for the rich and the poor. Although a man is rich, he can add nothing to this table. Should another be poor, he shall have no less honor because of his poverty in regard to the things which are here and belong to everyone without distinction.... The same table is prepared for the poor man, sitting waiting for an alms, as for the emperor, adorned with the diadem and clad in the royal purple, who rules the world. Such are the gifts of God. He gives not according to dignity but according to the will and mind of the one who receives. Therefore, let the poor man and the emperor come with equal confidence and with equal profit to this table.

As Christians we are brothers. At God's table we are all His children. Only one distinction is worth noting: that between the worthy and the unworthy. Examining our consciences for us, Saint John Chrysostom continues:

> Let those who possess a clean heart, a clear conscience, a way of living that is without reproach, come to the Lord's table. Those who are not of this kind, let them not come even once, for they take judgment and damnation to themselves. For just as food that has the power to nourish,

In the same way also the cup, after supper, saying, "This cup is the new covenant in my blood. Do this, as often as you drink it, in remembrance of me."

The new commandment

When he had gone out, Jesus said, "Now is the Son of man glorified, and in him God is glorified; if God is glorified in him, God will also glorify him in himself, and glorify him at once. Little children, yet a little while I am with you. You will seek me; and as I said to the Jews so now I say to you, 'Where I am going you cannot come.' A new commandment I give to you, that you love one another; even as I have loved you, that you also love one another. By this all men will know that you are my disciples, if you have love for one another."

JOHN 13:31-35

Peter's denials foretold

Then Jesus said to them, "You will all fall away because of me this night; for it is written, 'I will strike the shepherd, and the sheep of the flock will be scattered.' But after I am raised up, I will go before you to Galilee." Peter declared to him, "Though they all fall away because of you, I will never fall away." Jesus said to him, "Truly, I say to you, this very night, before the cock crows, you will deny me three times." Peter said to him, "Even if I must die with you, I will not deny you." And so said all the disciples.

MATTHEW 26:31-35

"Simon, Simon, behold, Satan demanded to have you, that he might sift you like wheat, but I have prayed for you that your faith may not fail; and when you have turned again, strengthen your brethren."

LUKE 22:31-32

Peter said to him, "Even though they all fall away, I will not." And Jesus said to him, "Truly, I say to you, this very night, before the cock crows twice, you will deny me three times." But he said vehemently, "If I must die with you, I will not deny you." And they all said the same.

MARK 14:29-31

Dangers and hardships shall try the apostles

And he said to them, "When I sent you out with no purse or bag or sandals, did you lack anything?" They said, "Nothing." He said to them, "But now,

LUKE 22:34b-38

if it is taken by one who has a stomach infested with disease, injures and aggravates everything and becomes a cause rather than a remedy of illness, so is it with this tremendous mystery. Will you partake of this spiritual table, the table of the King, and then soil your body again with filth? Do you anoint it with ointments, and then fill it up with foulness? Do you consider that it suffices for the forgiveness of the sins of the whole year if you at each returning year partake of Communion and then at the end of the week return to your former way of life? Tell me this. If after forty days you were restored to health from a serious illness, would you return to those things that earlier had caused your illness? Would you then not squander uselessly all your former efforts? If the things of the body are spoiled in this way, how much more so the things that depend on our own free will and decision?

Jesus' last discourse to His disciples.

let him who has a purse take it, and likewise a bag.
And let him who has no sword sell his mantle and
buy one. For I tell you that this scripture must be
fulfilled in me, 'And he was reckoned with transgressors'; for what is written about me has its ful-
filment." And they said, "Look, Lord, here are two
swords." And he said to them, "It is enough."

Words of comfort: promise of the Holy Spirit

JOHN 14:1-31

"Let not your hearts be troubled; believe in God,
believe also in me. In my Father's house are many
rooms; if it were not so, would I have told you that
I go to prepare a place for you? And when I go
and prepare a place for you, I will come again and
will take you to myself, that where I am you may
be also. And you know the way where I am going."
Thomas said to him, "Lord, we do not know where
you are going; how can we know the way?" Jesus
said to him, "I am the way, and the truth, and the
life; no one comes to the Father, but by me. If you
had known me, you would have known my Father
also; henceforth you know him and have seen him."
Philip said to him, "Lord, show us the Father,
and we shall be satisfied." Jesus said to him, "Have
I been with you so long, and yet you do not know
me, Philip? He who has seen me has seen the
Father; how can you say, 'Show us the Father'?
Do you not believe that I am in the Father and
the Father in me? The words that I say to you I
do not speak on my own authority; but the Father
who dwells in me does his works. Believe me that
I am in the Father and the Father in me; or else
believe me for the sake of the works themselves.
"Truly, truly, I say to you, he who believes in
me will also do the works that I do; and greater
works than these will he do, because I go to the
Father. Whatever you ask in my name, I will do it,
that the Father may be glorified in the Son; if you
ask anything in my name, I will do it.
"If you love me, you will keep my commandments.
And I will pray the Father, and he will give you
another Counselor, to be with you for ever, even
the Spirit of truth, whom the world cannot receive,
because it neither sees him nor knows him; you
know him, for he dwells with you, and will be in
you.

Holy Thursday is the night of divine love, the love which comes into our souls through Holy Communion. For love of us the Savior will die on the cross tomorrow. For love of us the Savior will rise from the dead on the third day. For love of us the Savior gives Himself as the life of each soul that might grow weary on its journey from the death of mortality to the life of immortality. This night, then, witnesses the example of divine love. Not content with merely giving us Himself, the Master wishes to show us the limitless proportions of His love. He stoops to wash the feet of His apostles. He literally descends to the depths of humility in order to show us how we might rise to the heights of glory. With Saint Augustine we exclaim:

> What a marvel it is that He pours water into a basin with which to wash the disciples' feet who shed His Blood upon the earth with which to wash out the filthiness of sin! What a marvel it is that with the towel with which He was girded He wiped the feet He had washed who by the flesh He had put on confirmed the footsteps of the evangelists.... About to become the victim of man's hatred, He first performed the lowly services of love, not only to them for whom He was about to suffer death, but even for him who was about to deliver Him up to death.... All of us men who were damned by following the pride of the deceiver are now saved by following the humility of the Redeemer.

Our humility, like the Savior's, must be wedded to love. When stripped of brotherly love, humility can lead one down the road of self-righteous pride. Joined to Christian love, humility forces the Christian soul to empty self of self to such a degree that there can be room only for the goodness of God. From Christ's example of washing His apostles' feet, Saint Augustine draws another lesson for us:

> Let us forgive each others' sins, and for our own sins pray for each other. In doing this we shall, as it were, wash one another's feet. It is our duty to perform the ministry of charity and humility. It is Christ's pleasure to hear our prayers and cleanse us from all contamination of sin. In this way, by forgiving each other, what is loosed on earth will be loosed also in heaven.

The scenes on Holy Thursday night change swiftly. Christ leaves the upper room and converses with His apostles as they pass through the holy city, cross the brook called Cedron, and enter the Garden of Olives. He picks out three — Peter, James, and John — and goes further on to enter into the bitter prelude to His passion, the agony in the garden. Saint John Chrysostom finds a spiritual meaning in the very name of the Mount of Olives. His meaning harks back to the divine commandment of Christian love:

> Let us also go out unto the hands of the poor, for this is the meaning of the Mount of Olives. The multitude of the poor are olive-trees planted in the house of God, dropping down oil which is profitable for us. This is the oil the five virgins had, and the others who did not have it, perished. Having received this oil because of our gifts to the poor, let us enter in with lamps glowing in order to meet the divine Bridegroom.

"I will not leave you desolate; I will come to you. Yet a little while, and the world will see me no more, but you will see me; because I live, you will live also. In that day you will know that I am in my Father, and you in me, and I in you. He who has my commandments and keeps them, he it is who loves me; and he who loves me will be loved by my Father, and I will love him and manifest myself to him." Judas (not Iscariot) said to him, "Lord, how is it that you will manifest yourself to us, and not to the world?" Jesus answered him, "If a man loves me, he will keep my word, and my Father will love him, and we will come to him and make our home with him. He who does not love me does not keep my words; and the word which you hear is not mine but the Father's who sent me.

"These things I have spoken to you, while I am still with you. But the Counselor, the Holy Spirit, whom the Father will send in my name, he will teach you all things, and bring to your remembrance all that I have said to you. Peace I leave with you; my peace I give to you; not as the world gives do I give to you. Let not your hearts be troubled, neither let them be afraid. You heard me say to you, 'I go away, and I will come to you.' If you loved me, you would have rejoiced, because I go to the Father; for the Father is greater than I. And now I have told you before it takes place, so that when it does take place, you may believe. I will no longer talk much with you, for the ruler of this world is coming. He has no power over me; but I do as the Father has commanded me, so that the world may know that I love the Father. Rise, let us go hence.

Union with Christ

JOHN 15:1-17

"I am the true vine, and my Father is the vine-dresser. Every branch of mine that bears no fruit, he takes away, and every branch that does bear fruit he prunes, that it may bear more fruit. You are already made clean by the word which I have spoken to you. Abide in me, and I in you. As the branch cannot bear fruit by itself, unless it abides in the vine, neither can you, unless you abide in me. I am the vine, you are the branches. He who abides in me, and I in him, he it is that bears much fruit,

Here on the Mount of Olives Christ suffers His bloody agony, in so many ways more painful than the blows that would be showered upon His earthly body in the coming hours. Here pass before His mind's eye all the sins of mankind until the end of time. Here He sees the sufferings of His Mystical Body, how one member would inflict suffering on another, how one member would set about to destroy himself and others. Here Christ views the sins of all mankind, the sins of the high and mighty, the sins of all the unknowns of history. Christ sees all the sins of the world, your sins, my sins. Christ sees, and His whole body perspires with great drops of blood. From the agony in the garden Dionysius of Alexandria draws these lessons for our meditation:

> By voluntarily enduring the death in the flesh, He implanted incorruptibility in it. So also, by taking on Himself of His own free will the sufferings of human nature, He set in us the seeds of constancy and courage. Thus He has equipped those who believe in Him for the mighty conflicts belonging to their witness-bearing. Those drops of sweat flowed from Him in a marvellous manner, like great drops of blood, in order that He might, as it were, drain off and empty the fountain of fear that is proper to our human nature. Also important is that sentence in the narrative which tells us that an angel stood by the Savior and strengthened Him. For this, too, is related to our salvation, inasmuch as those who are appointed to engage in the sacred struggles of conflict for the sake of religion have the angels from heaven to assist them.

The heavenly Father sent an angel to comfort Christ when His own apostles abandoned Him, and Judas heeded the Master's admonition: "What you are going to do, do quickly" (John 13:27). Saint Leo the Great explains the expression:

> This is the voice of permission, not of command, of readiness, not of fear. He who has power over all time, shows that He does not hinder the traitor in his work. Rather, He carries out the Father's will for the redemption of the world in such a way that He neither promoted nor feared the crime which His persecutors were preparing.

All this time Judas was busy performing his evil deed. In the darkness of the night he carried out his task, for so hideous was that secret mission to the chief priests that shame forbade its execution in the light of day. For thirty pieces of silver, a pittance, Judas was willing to betray the Lord of the world. Greed entered his heart. No future, unknown kingdom for him. Judas wanted power *now*. He craved glory *now*. He reached out to grasp riches *now*. To all the lesser Judases of all times who would exchange the Lord of the world for the creatures of His earth, Saint John Chrysostom gives warning:

> Hear, you covetous ones, and consider what happened to Judas. At one and the same time he lost the money, committed the crime, and destroyed his own soul. Such is the tyranny of covetousness. Judas enjoyed the money neither in this present life nor in the life to come, but at one and the same time lost both lives. Despised by the men who gave him the money, he went out and hanged himself.

for apart from me you can do nothing. If a man does not abide in me, he is cast forth as a branch and withers; and the branches are gathered, thrown into the fire and burned. If you abide in me, and my words abide in you, ask whatever you will, and it shall be done for you. By this my Father is glorified, that you bear much fruit, and so prove to be my disciples. As the Father has loved me, so have I loved you; abide in my love. If you keep my commandments, you will abide in my love, just as I have kept my Father's commandments and abide in his love. These things I have spoken to you, that my joy may be in you, and that your joy may be full.

"This is my commandment, that you love one another as I have loved you. Greater love has no man than this, that a man lay down his life for his friends. You are my friends if you do what I command you. No longer do I call you servants, for the servant does not know what his master is doing; but I have called you friends, for all that I have heard from my Father I have made known to you. You did not choose me, but I chose you and appointed you that you should go and bear fruit and that your fruit should abide; so that whatever you ask the Father in my name, he may give it to you. This I command you, to love one another.

The world's hatred

JOHN 15:18-27

"If the world hates you, know that it has hated me before it hated you. If you were of the world, the world would love its own; but because you are not of the world, but I chose you out of the world, therefore the world hates you. Remember the word that I said to you. 'A servant is not greater than his master.' If they persecuted me, they will persecute you; if they kept my word, they will keep yours also. But all this they will do to you on my account, because they do not know him who sent me. If I had not come and spoken to them, they would not have sin; but now they have no excuse for their sin. He who hates me hates my Father also. If I had not done among them the works which no one else did, they would not have sin; but now they have seen and hated both me and my Father. It is to fulfil the word that is written

Judas' tragedy did not come about in one moment. Who can say when he began to turn from Christ? Who can say when any sinner begins his downward path, turning from the friendship of Christ to the ugliness of selfish desires? When did Judas stop listening to the merciful words of a loving Savior? When does the sinner begin to turn deaf ears to the same loving words of the same loving Savior? Judas, says Saint Leo the Great,

> never seriously reflected upon the proofs of the Savior's mercy. His ears had heard the Lord's words when He said, "I came not to call the righteous, but sinners," and also, "The Son of man came to seek and to save that which was lost." But these words did not pierce Judas' understanding. The mercy of Christ not only healed bodily infirmities but also the wounds of sick souls, saying to the paralytic man, "Take heart, my son; your sins are forgiven," and saying to the adulteress who was brought to him, "Neither will I condemn you; go and sin no more." In all His works He showed that He had come as the Savior, not the judge, of the world.

Even from Judas we can learn lessons which will help us draw closer to the Savior he betrayed. Christ did not exclude Judas from His all-embracing love. Even though as God He knew that Judas was plotting His destruction, He loved him and had compassion on him. Up to the very last moment the Savior still hoped and prayed for Judas' conversion. Marveling at this goodness, Dionysius of Alexandria exclaims:

> How full of wonder is this endurance of evil by the Lord, who even kissed the traitor and spoke words softer even than the kiss! He did not say, "O abominable, utterly abominable, traitor, is this the return you make for so many kindnesses?" Rather than being angry with him, He simply says, "Judas," using the proper name which was the address that would be used by one who has compassion on a person . . . . Blessed art thou, O Lord! How great is this example of the endurance of evil that you have shown us in your own person! How great, too, the example of humility! The Lord has given us this example to show us that we ought not to give up offering our good counsel to our brethren, even should nothing remarkable result from our words.

Never-ending, never-tiring love of God and neighbor is the first lesson we can apply to ourselves from the story of Judas. Saint Basil also draws a lesson of perseverance from the traitor's sorry plight:

> Surely enough of an example for all who are living a holy life is the fall from the better to the worse in the case of Judas. After being Christ's disciple for so long a time, Judas sold his Master for a paltry sum and then hung himself with a halter. Learn then, brother, that it is not he who begins well who is perfect. Rather, he who carries the work out to completion gains God's approval.

At this very moment Peter was comfortably sleeping — Peter who boasted so proudly that he would die for the Master. Peter, chosen to be the leader, tricked by his own pride. We must agree with Saint Augustine:

> It does not please us to accuse the chief of the apostles. But in considering his action, we ought to realize more deeply that no man should

in their law, 'They hated me without a cause.' But when the Counselor comes, whom I shall send to you from the Father, even the Spirit of truth, who proceeds from the Father, he will bear witness to me; and you also are witnesses, because you have been with me from the beginning.

Persecution foretold

JOHN 16:1-5

"I have said all this to you to keep you from falling away. They will put you out of the synagogues; indeed, the hour is coming when whoever kills you will think he is offering service to God. And they will do this because they have not known the Father, nor me. But I have said these things to you, that when their hour comes you may remember that I told you of them.

"I did not say these things to you from the beginning, because I was with you. But now I am going to him who sent me; yet none of you asks me, 'Where are you going?'

The role of the Advocate: necessity of Christ's departure: joy after sorrow

JOHN 16:6-33

"But because I have said these things to you, sorrow has filled your hearts. Nevertheless I tell you the truth: it is to your advantage that I go away, for if I do not go away, the Counselor will not come to you; but if I go, I will send him to you. And when he comes, he will convince the world of sin and of righteousness and of judgment: of sin, because they do not believe in me; of righteousness, because I go to the Father, and you will see me no more; of judgment, because the ruler of this world is judged.

"I have yet many things to say to you, but you cannot bear them now. When the Spirit of truth comes, he will guide you into all the truth; for he will not speak on his own authority, but whatever he hears he will speak, and he will declare to you the things that are to come. He will glorify me, for he will take what is mine and declare it to you. All that the Father has is mine; therefore I said that he will take what is mine and declare it to you.

"A little while, and you will see me no more; again a little while, and you will see me." Some of his disciples said to one another, "What is this that he trust in his own strength. What other reason had our Teacher and Savior than to show us by the example of the very chief of the apostles that no man should presume upon his own powers in any circumstance?

To be sure, Peter was weak; he had not yet received the strength and power of the Holy Spirit. In later ages martyrs by the thousands would gladly die for the sake of Christ. But they were able to do so chiefly because they had received "power from on high." With this thought in mind we can more readily understand this comparison Saint John Chrysostom makes between Peter and Judas:

> A man's willingness is not sufficient unless he receives help from above. On the other hand, help from above will be of little value if a man is unwilling. Peter and Judas show both these lessons. Judas, in spite of receiving much help, failed because he was unwilling to contribute anything on his own. Peter, though he was generous of soul, received little assistance and thus fell. Virtue's web is woven from divine assistance and human cooperation.

Neither Judas nor Peter, however, could stop the development of events this sacred night. Christ's seizure in the garden, His scourging, crowning with thorns, buffeting, and ridicule were pre-ordained. He entered into His passion not because of the deceits, the denial, or the cunning of men, but because of the power these sufferings would have to deliver men from their sins. Saint Cyril of Jerusalem points out that even the crown of thorns has meaning for us:

> Adam received the doom:
> "Cursed is the ground because of you . . . thorns and thistles it shall bring forth to you." For this reason Jesus assumes the thorns, that He might cancel the doom. For this reason also He was buried in the earth, that the cursed earth might receive instead of the curse a blessing.

The crown of thorns symbolized for many of the early Church Fathers the removal of the curse upon the earth. Just as through Adam's sin all creation suffered with man, so now through Christ's redemption all nature would be renewed and restored. In the words of Rufinus:

> It was appropriate that He who came to remove the sins of the world should also release the earth from the curses inflicted on it when the first man sinned . . . . Jesus was, therefore, crowned with thorns in order that the primordial sentence of condemnation might be remitted. He was led to the cross and the life of the whole world hung suspended from its wood.

It was, indeed, fitting also that on this sacred night Christ should be crowned, even if with thorns. No one knew better than He that in reality He was the victor and His persecutors the vanquished. Even during these hours of shame and blasphemy Christ remained the Master. The mockery of the soldiers who crowned Him with thorns and placed a reed in His hands and cried out, "Hail! our King!" unwittingly proclaimed the truth and fulfilled the prophecies. Thus Rufinus continues:

> In order to accomplish salvation through the weakness of the flesh, His divine nature succumbed to the death of the flesh. The reason was

says to us, 'A little while, and you will not see me,
and again a little while, and you will see me'; and,
'because I go to the Father'? They said, "What does
he mean by 'a little while'? We do not know what
he means." Jesus knew that they wanted to ask
him; so he said to them, "Is this what you are
asking yourselves, what I meant by saying, 'A little
while, and you will not see me, and again a little
while, and you will see me'? Truly, truly, I say to
you, you will weep and lament, but the world will
rejoice; you will be sorrowful, but your sorrow will
turn into joy. When a woman is in travail she has
sorrow, because her hour has come; but when she
is delivered of the child, she no longer remembers
the anguish, for joy that a child is born into the
world. So you have sorrow now, but I will see you
again and your hearts will rejoice, and no one will
take your joy from you. In that day you will ask
me no questions. Truly, truly, I say to you, if you
ask anything of the Father, he will give it to you
in my name. Hitherto you have asked nothing in
my name; ask, and you will receive, that your joy
may be full.

"I have said this to you in figures; the hour is
coming when I shall no longer speak to you in
figures but tell you plainly of the Father. In that
day you will ask in my name; and I do not say
to you that I shall pray the Father for you; for the
Father himself loves you, because you have loved
me and have believed that I came from the Father.
I came from the Father and have come into the
world; again, I am leaving the world and going to
the Father."

His disciples said, "Ah, now you are speaking
plainly, not in any figure! Now we know that you
know all things, and need none to question you;
by this we believe that you came from God." Jesus
answered them, "Do you now believe? The hour
is coming, indeed it has come, when you will be
scattered, every man to his home, and will leave
me alone; yet I am not alone, for the Father is
with me. I have said this to you, that in me you
may have peace. In the world you have tribulation;
but be of good cheer, I have overcome the world."

Christ's priestly prayer

JOHN 17:1-26

When Jesus had spoken these words, he lifted up
his eyes to heaven and said, "Father, the hour has

that, rather than being conquered by death as are all human beings, He would destroy the gates of death through the assurance that He would rise again by His own power. He was as a king who goes down into the dungeon and there throws open its doors, unties the bonds, breaks the chains, bolts and bars in pieces and leads the captives out to freedom.... In such a case the king is, of course, in the dungeon, but not under the same circumstances· as the prisoners who are confined there. They are there because of their offenses. He enters there in order to free them from their punishments.

This sacred night fulfills many prophecies written about the Messiah. In order to fulfill these sacred words, Christ willingly undergoes every imaginable suffering. Tertullian comments:

He even knows the very time that it is fitting for Him to suffer because the ancient law prefigured His passion. Thus, of all the festive days of the Jews he chooses the Passover... because He was to be "like a lamb that is led to the slaughter.".... In a similar way He might have been betrayed by any stranger, but even here He fulfilled the words of the psalmist: "Even my bosom friend in whom I trusted, who ate of my bread, has lifted his heel against Me." He might also have been betrayed without a price being fixed on His head. Although this might have sufficed in other cases, it would not have been acceptable to Him who was consciously fulfilling the prophecies. It is written: "They sell the righteous one for silver." The very amount and the final usage of the money, as narrated in the Gospel of Saint Matthew, was clearly foretold by Jeremias.

Explaining this desire of Christ to fulfill the prophecies, Saint Leo the Great remarks:

Things which had long been promised under mysterious figures had now to be fulfilled in all clearness. For instance, the true Sheep had to supercede the sheep which were its prototypes, and the one Sacrifice had to bring to an end the multitude of different sacrifices. For all those things which had been divinely ordained through Moses about the sacrifice of the lamb had foreshadowed Christ and truly announced the slaying of Christ. Therefore, in order that the shadows should yield to the substance and types cease in the presence of reality, the ancient observances are removed by the new sacrament, the ancient victims give way to the true Victim, the ancient blood of goats is wiped away by His Blood, and the law-ordained feast of the Passover is fulfilled by being transformed.

These are, to be sure, reasons for the blasphemies inflicted upon the sacred Body of our divine Savior. They are not. however, the chief reason. He endured all these bitter sufferings of this lonely night because He loved us. That tremendous love of the Son of God for His brothers on earth prompted Him to endure all pain, undergo all sufferings, not only willingly and freely, but even joyfully. because He realized this was the price for the salvation of all men. "Do you know why this friend of mankind did not shun death?" Saint Cyril of Jerusalem asks. Then he answers:

come; glorify thy Son that the Son may glorify thee, since thou hast given him power over all flesh, to give eternal life to all whom thou hast given him. And this is eternal life, that they know thee the only true God, and Jesus Christ whom thou hast sent. I glorified thee on earth, having accomplished the work which thou gavest me to do; and now, Father, glorify thou me in thy own presence with the glory which I had with thee before the world was made.

"I have manifested thy name to the men whom thou gavest me out of the world; thine they were, and thou gavest them to me, and they have kept thy word. Now they know that everything that thou hast given me is from thee; for I have given them the words which thou gavest me, and they have received them and know in truth that I came from thee; and they have believed that thou didst send me. I am praying for them; I am not praying for the world but for those whom thou hast given me, for they are thine; all mine are thine, and thine are mine, and I am glorified in them. And now I am no more in the world, but they are in the world, and I am coming to thee. Holy Father, keep them in thy name which thou hast given me, that they may be one, even as we are one. While I was with them, I kept them in thy name which thou hast given me; I have guarded them, and none of them is lost but the son of perdition, that the scripture might be fulfilled. But now I am coming to thee; and these things I speak in the world, that they may have my joy fulfilled in themselves. I have given them thy word; and the world has hated them because they are not of the world, even as I am not of the world. I do not pray that thou shouldst take them out of the world, but that thou shouldst keep them from the evil one. They are not of the world, even as I am not of the world. Sanctify them in the truth; thy word is truth. As thou didst send me into the world, so I have sent them into the world. And for their sake I consecrate myself, that they also may be consecrated in truth.

"I do not pray for these only, but also for those who are to believe in me through their word, that they may all be one; even as thou, Father, art in me, and I in thee, that they also may be in us, so that the world may believe that thou hast sent me. The glory which thou hast given me I have

It was because He did not wish to see the whole world perish in its sins. He neither surrendered His life by force nor did He die violently, but freely of His own will. For He Himself said, "I have power to lay it (my life) down and I have power to take it again." He therefore entered upon His passion of His own will, rejoicing in His noble deed, smiling at the crown of thorns, being cheered by the salvation of men, and not ashamed of the cross for by it He saved the world.

Earlier this sacred night Christ spoke tender words of love to His apostles. Now, alone and forsaken by men, even the men whom He loved above all others, He enters into the furnace of man's hatred in order to prove His love for all men, foes as well as friends. Truly, this is the night of love. This is our example: "Greater love than this no man has than that a man lay down his life for his friends."

This is the night of the Eucharist. The words of Saint Paul echo in our ears: "We are members of His Body." And as we return to our homes we will recall that other question: "Do you not know that your bodies are members of Christ?" (1 Cor. 6:15).

given to them, that they may be one even as we are one, I in them and thou in me, that they may become perfectly one, so that the world may know that thou hast sent me and hast loved them even as thou hast loved me. Father, I desire that they also, whom thou hast given me, may be with me where I am, to behold my glory which thou hast given me in thy love for me before the foundation of the world. O righteous Father, the world has not known thee, but I have known thee; and these know that thou hast sent me. I made known to them thy name, and I will make it known, that the love with which thou hast loved me may be in them, and I in them."

GOOD FRIDAY

Grief. Black, stark, naked grief. In a way, the whole world stands aghast at the tragedy of this day. We sense this grief in the stillness of nature, in the embarrassed silence of men.

We call this day simply "Good Friday" because on this day Goodness died to make all men good. The price of our virtue is the death of Him who is virtue. Terrible thought! The price of human goodness is infinite Goodness! All good men are His debtors.

In a very real sense, we caused His death. We fashioned the cross. We stood beneath that cross; our sins drove the nails deeper into His sacred flesh, pushed down the crown of thorns deeper on His sacred head. The death of our sins demanded His death. We can rise from sin only when He shall incorporate us into His resurrection.

And so today we weep. We weep for our sins because we know now what they have caused. We weep, too, for our loving Savior, not so much because He needs our sorrow, but rather because we are the guilty ones who have rebuked His love. Today we live in the shadow of His cross. Today we must remain there to satisfy infinite love, to be one with the Savior in His death for, paradoxically, His death is the threshold of our life. As Saint Ambrose told his people in Milan:

> His death is the life of all. We are signed with the sign of His death. We show forth His death when we pray. We declare His death when we offer the Sacrifice. His death is victory. His death is our mystery. His death is the annual recurring solemnity of the world.

Today we belong on Calvary, called Golgotha, "the place of the skull," by the Evangelist. Even the name has meaning for us. Here all history converges. Here time finds its fulfillment. Here each of us discovers the purpose of his life. Here Christ fulfills His own words: "And I, when I am lifted up from the earth, will draw all men to Myself" (John 12:32). Reflecting on the "place of the skull," Saint Cyril of Jerusalem draws this lesson for our consideration:

THE PASSION AND DEATH OF JESUS

GETHSEMANE

Christ enters the garden with His apostles

JOHN 18:1

When Jesus had spoken these words, he went forth with his disciples across the Kidron valley, where there was a garden, which he and his disciples entered.

His agony and bloody sweat

MATTHEW 26:36-46

Then Jesus went with them to a place called Gethsemane, and he said to his disciples, "Sit here, while I go yonder and pray." And taking with him Peter and the two sons of Zebedee, he began to be sorrowful and troubled. Then he said to them, "My soul is very sorrowful, even to death; remain here, and watch with me." And going a little farther he fell on his face and prayed, "My Father, if it be possible, let this cup pass from me; nevertheless, not as I will, but as thou wilt." And he came to the disciples and found them sleeping; and he said to Peter, "So, could you not watch with me one hour? Watch and pray that you may not enter into temptation; the spirit indeed is willing, but the flesh is weak." Again, for the second time, he went away and prayed, "My Father, if this cannot pass unless I drink it, thy will be done." And again he came and found them sleeping, for their eyes were heavy. So, leaving them again, he went away and prayed for the third time, saying the same words.

Jesus asks His disciples to watch with Him.

Then he came to the disciples and said to them, "Are you still sleeping and taking your rest? Behold, **the hour is at hand, and the Son** of man is betrayed into the hands of sinners. Rise, let us be going; see, my betrayer is at hand."

The kiss of Judas: the arrest

MATTHEW 26:47-56

While he was still speaking, Judas came, one of the twelve, and with him a great crowd with swords and clubs, from the chief priests and the elders of the people. Now the betrayer had given them a sign, saying, "The one I shall kiss is the man; seize him." And he came up to Jesus at once and said, "Hail, Master!" And he kissed him. Jesus said to him, "Friend, why are you here?" Then they came up and laid hands on Jesus and seized him. And behold, one of those who were with Jesus stretched out his hand and drew his sword, and struck the slave of the high priest, and cut off his ear. Then Jesus said to him, "Put your sword back into its place; for all who take the sword will perish by the sword. Do you think that I cannot appeal to my Father, and he will at once send me more than twelve legions of angels? But how then should the scriptures be fulfilled, that it must be so?" At that hour Jesus said to the crowds, "Have you come out as against a robber, with swords and clubs to capture me? Day after day I sat in the temple teaching, and you did not seize me. But all this has taken place, that the scriptures of the prophets might be fulfilled." Then all the disciples forsook him and fled.

THE TRIAL OF CHRIST

Jesus before Annas

JOHN 18:13

First they led him to Annas; for he was the father-in-law of Caiaphas, who was high priest that year.

He stretched out His hands on the cross in order to encompass the ends of the world, for Golgotha is the very center of the earth. Not I, but a prophet, has said: "Thou hast accomplished salvation in the middle of the earth." He who established the heavens with spiritual hands, now stretches forth human hands. They are fastened with nails to show that His humanity carries the sins of men. They are nailed to the tree so that when He dies, sin dies; and we all might rise again in holiness.

Here on Golgotha we stand today, contemplating the cruel death of our Savior. Here we belong, not because we are saints but because we are sinners. In fact, the more we have sinned, the longer we should stand here contemplating the sufferings and death of our Savior. Nor can any sinner be out of place at this holy altar of the cross for, as Saint Prosper of Aquitaine remarked,

There can be no reason to doubt that Jesus died for unbelievers and sinners. If there had been anyone who was not one or the other, then Christ would not have died for all. But He did die for all men without exception. There is no one, therefore, in the whole human race who was not, before the reconciliation that Christ brought about by shedding His Blood, either a sinner or an unbeliever.

Standing here beneath His cross, we realize that we are not alone. At every great moment in the life of the Church, as well as in the lives of her members, we find that our companion is the Mother of God. She stands beneath Christ's cross today as His helper and ours. She offers her divine Son consolation; she tenders all her children loving solicitude. Although she weeps (and teaches us that we too must weep), she looks to the future with holy hope and urges us to do the same. Saint Ambrose describes the Blessed Mother beneath the cross:

When the apostles fled, she stood beneath the cross and with pious eyes beheld her Son's wounds. She did not consider the death of her divine Son as much as the salvation of the world. Perhaps because she knew that the redemption of the world would be through the death of her Son she thought that by her death also she might add something to the common good. Jesus, however, who saved all of us without a helper, did not need a helper now . . . . He received, indeed, the affection of His mother but sought no other's help.

With Mary we begin to comprehend the marvellous exchange taking place before our eyes. "The Lord trembled with our fear," says Saint Leo the Great,

in order that He might fully clothe our weakness and fraility with the fulness of His own strength. He came into this world as a rich and merciful merchant from heaven and here bargains for our salvation. He receives our lives in exchange for His, our insults for His honor, our salvation for His pains, our lives for His death.

No one understood so well the nature of this divine exchange as the good thief. He, too, is with us on Golgotha. He came, it is true, at first unwillingly; but now, as he contemplates the great sacrifice taking place

Jesus before the Sanhedrin: the charge of blasphemy

MARK 14:53-64

And they led Jesus to the high priest; and all the chief priests and the elders and the scribes were assembled. And Peter had followed him at a distance, right into the courtyard of the high priest; and he was sitting with the guards, and warming himself at the fire. Now the chief priests and the whole council sought testimony against Jesus to put him to death; but they found none. For many bore false witness against him, and their witness did not agree. And some stood up and bore false witness against him, saying, "We heard him say, 'I will destroy this temple that is made with hands, and in three days I will build another, not made with hands.'" Yet not even so did their testimony agree. And the high priest stood up in the midst, and asked Jesus, "Have you no answer to make? What is it that these men testify against you?" But he was silent and made no answer. Again the high priest asked him, "Are you the Christ, the Son of the Blessed?" And Jesus said, "I am; and you will see the Son of man sitting at the right hand of Power, and coming with the clouds of heaven." And the high priest tore his mantle, and said, "Why do we still need witnesses? You have heard his blasphemy. What is your decision?" And they all condemned him as deserving death.

Peter's denials

MARK 14:66-72

And as Peter was below in the courtyard, one of the maids of the high priest came; and seeing Peter warming himself, she looked at him, and said, "You also were with the Nazarene, Jesus." But he denied it, saying, "I neither know nor understand what you mean." And he went out into the gateway. And the maid saw him, and began again to say to the bystanders, "This man is one of them." But again he denied it. And after a little while again the bystanders said to Peter, "Certainly you are one of them; for you are a Galilean." But he began to invoke a curse on himself and to swear, "I do not know this man of whom you speak." And immediately the cock crowed a second time. And Peter remembered how Jesus had said to him, "Before the cock crows twice, you will deny me three times." And he broke down and wept.

Jesus foretells Peter's denial.

It was Caiaphas who had given counsel to the Jews
that it was expedient that one man should die for
the people.

Simon Peter followed Jesus, and so did another
disciple. As this disciple was known to the high
priest, he entered the court of the high priest along
with Jesus while Peter stood outside at the door.
So the other disciple, who was known to the high
priest, went out and spoke to the maid who kept
the door, and brought Peter in. The maid who
kept the door said to Peter, "Are not you also one
of this man's disciples?" He said, "I am not." Now
the servants and officers had made a charcoal fire,
because it was cold, and they were standing and
warming themselves; Peter also was with them,
standing and warming himself.

The high priest then questioned Jesus about his
disciples and his teaching. Jesus answered him,
"I have spoken openly to the world; I have always
taught in synagogues and in the temple, where all
Jews come together; I have said nothing secretly.
Why do you ask me? Ask those who have heard
me, what I said to them; they know what I said."
When he had said this, one of the officers standing
by struck Jesus with his hand, saying, "Is that how
you answer the high priest?" Jesus answered him,
"If I have spoken wrongly, bear witness to the
wrong; but if I have spoken rightly, why do you
strike me?" Annas then sent him bound to Caiaphas
the high priest.

Now Simon Peter was standing and warming himself. They said to him, "Are not you also one of his
disciples?" He denied it and said, "I am not." One
of the servants of the high priest, a kinsman of the
man whose ear Peter had cut off, asked, "Did I
not see you in the garden with him?" Peter again
denied it; and at once the cock crowed.

Jesus is mocked and maltreated

Now the men who were holding Jesus mocked
him and beat him; they also blindfolded him and
asked him, "Prophesy! Who is it that struck you?"
And they spoke many other words against him,
reviling him.

Jesus is led to be condemned.

Second hearing before the Sanhedrin:
Jesus is condemned

LUKE 22:66-71

When day came, the assembly of the elders of the people gathered together, both chief priests and scribes; and they led him away to their council, and they said, "If you are the Christ, tell us." But he said to them, "If I tell you, you will not believe; and if I ask you, you will not answer. But from now on the Son of man shall be seated at the right hand of the power of God." And they all said, "Are you the Son of God, then?" And he said to them, "You say that I am." And they said, "What further testimony do we need? We have heard it ourselves from his own lips."

Despair and suicide of Judas

MATTHEW 27:3-10

When Judas, his betrayer, saw that he was condemned, he repented and brought back the thirty pieces of silver to the chief priests and the elders, saying, "I have sinned in betraying innocent blood." They said, "What is that to us? See to it yourself." And throwing down the pieces of silver in the temple, he departed; and he went and hanged himself. But the chief priests, taking the pieces of silver, said, "It is not lawful to put them into the treasury, since they are blood money." So they took counsel, and bought with them the potter's field, to bury strangers in. Therefore that field has been called the Field of Blood to this day. Then was fulfilled what had been spoken by the prophet Jeremiah, saying, "And they took the thirty pieces of silver, the price of him on whom a price had been set by some of the sons of Israel, and they gave them for the potter's field, as the Lord directed me."

Jesus before Pilate

JOHN 18:28

Then they led Jesus from the house of Caiaphas to the praetorium. It was early. They themselves did not enter the praetorium, so that they might not be defiled, but might eat the passover.

The Jews accuse Christ:
the questioning and indecision of Pilate

JOHN 18:29-38

So Pilate went out to them and said, "What accusation do you bring against this man?" They

before his eyes, he becomes the first to experience the Savior's merciful redemption. "Be of good cheer," the Savior tells him. How well he knew that his actions did not deserve to make him cheerful. Rather, he knew, as Mary knew beneath the cross, the King was here dispensing favors. He knew, too, that his request concerning the future would be answered, just as he knew that divine grace was already working in his heart. Addressing his remarks to the good thief, Saint Cyril of Jerusalem says: "Adam fell from paradise by the tree; you are brought to paradise by the tree."

Like Mary we must unite ourselves with Christ in His death, to show Him that we are willing to be His helpers in carrying out the work of saving of the world. Like the good thief we must confess our guilt; then we too shall be able to live with the holy hope that the Savior will remember us when He enters His Kingdom.

There is another exchange taking place before our eyes: Christ's return of goodness for the evil of His tormentors. Lest we judge too harshly those who actually tormented Christ in His physical body, we hang our own heads in shame, for we, by our sins, continue to torment Christ in His Mystical Body. What cruel men did here on Calvary by their own ignorance, we who are enlightened by faith continue to do by our evil deeds. This is the exchange that Saint Cyprian discusses:

> He who but a short time before had cured the eyes of the blind man with His own spittle is now covered with the spittle of His persecutors. He who now crowns the martyrs with eternal garlands is now crowned with thorns. He who now gives true palms to the victors is beaten in the face with hostile palms. He who now clothes all others with the garment of immortality is stripped of His earthly garments. He who now gives the food of heaven is fed gall. He who now offers us the cup of salvation is given vinegar to drink. He who is innocence is counted among criminals. He who is truth is accused by false testimonies.... The stars are stupefied by the crucifixion of the Lord, the elements disturbed, the earth shattered, night blots out the day, the sun withdraws both its rays and its eyes lest it be forced to gaze upon the crime of the Jews. All this time He does not speak, He does not proclaim His majesty. He endures all things, even to the bitter end, with constant perseverance so that in Him a full and perfect patience may find realization.

It is but human for us to ask why Christ the Son of God should subject Himself to these bitter offenses. Alexander of Alexandria answers the query simply: "Christ suffered that we should live forever.... For our sakes He endured sorrow, ignominy, torment, even death itself and burial." Saint Caesarius sees in the Savior's death an example of humility for all of us to follow. "If anyone wants to be a disciple of Christ," he says, "he should keep His commandments and love humility as He himself said: 'Learn of Me for I am meek and humble of heart.'" Saint Polycarp proposes the Savior's example for our imitation: "Let us become imitators of His patient endurance and, if we suffer anything for His sake, let us praise Him." Saint Leo the Great points to the Savior's willing resignation:

answered him, "If this man were not an evildoer, we would not have handed him over." Pilate said to them, "Take him yourselves and judge him by your own law." The Jews said to him, "It is not lawful for us to put any man to death." This was to fulfil the word which Jesus had spoken to show by what death he was to die.

Pilate entered the praetorium again and called Jesus, and said to him, "Are you the King of the Jews?" Jesus answered, "Do you say this of your own accord, or did others say it to you about me?" Pilate answered, "Am I a Jew? Your own nation and the chief priests have handed you over to me; what have you done?" Jesus answered, "My kingship is not of this world, my servants would fight, that I might not be handed over to the Jews; but my kingship is not from the world." Pilate said to him, "So you are a king?" Jesus answered, "You say that I am a king. For this I was born, and for this I have come into the world, to bear witness to the truth. Every one who is of the truth hears my voice." Pilate said to him, "What is truth?"

After he had said this, he went out to the Jews again, and told them, "I find no crime in him."

Jesus before Herod Antipas

LUKE 23:6-12

When Pilate heard this, he asked whether the man was a Galilean. And when he learned that he belonged to Herod's jurisdiction, he sent him over to Herod, who was himself in Jerusalem at that time. When Herod saw Jesus, he was very glad, for he had long desired to see him, because he had heard about him, and he was hoping to see some sign done by him. So he questioned him at some length; but he made no answer. The chief priests and the scribes stood by, vehemently accusing him. And Herod with his soldiers treated him with contempt and mocked him; then, arraying him in gorgeous apparel, he sent him back to Pilate. And Herod and Pilate became friends with each other that very day, for before this they had been at enmity with each other.

Pilate declares Christ's innocence

LUKE 23:13-16

Pilate then called together the chief priests and the rulers and the people, and said to them, "You

Who could overcome the world's hatred, the allurement of temptations, the terrors of persecutors, had not Christ, in our name and for our sake, said to the Father: "Thy will be done"? Let these words be learned by all the Church's sons who have been purchased at so great a price. When the shock of some violent temptation assails them, let them use the aid of this potent prayer that they may conquer their fear and trembling and learn to suffer patiently.

In His death Christ faced His finest hour. At this moment, says Saint Augustine,

An example was given the martyrs to bear all the sufferings that persecutors would impose upon them. By concealing His aweful power for a little while, Christ commended His patience to be imitated for all time. His Kingdom, which was not to be of this world, overcame the proud world, not through fierce fighting but through humble suffering. The grain of wheat which was to be multiplied was sown in horrible disgrace and would sprout forth in marvellous glory.

All during this time He remains our Leader, Savior, Sovereign, the Lord. So Saint Cyprian draws this lesson:

If it can be done, let us follow Him. Under His sacrament and sign let us be counted. He opens for us the way of life; He leads us back to paradise; He guides us to the kingdom of heaven. Having become sons of God through Him, we shall always live with Him. Having been restored by His Blood, we shall always rejoice with Him.

Expressing the same thought, Saint Augustine says pointedly: "Crucify your sins, that you may die to sin. He who dies to sin lives for God. Thus you should live for Him who spared not even His own Son. For Christ died for us that we might live in His revivified Body."

His consummation is our commencement. He gladly hangs on the cross today because He knows He shall rule from the same cross for endless ages. *Crux infama, crux gemmata*: The cross of shame becomes the cross of glory! Today He willingly endures all sufferings and blasphemies because these are the price of our salvation. He hides His divinity so that through His humanity He may draw all of us closer to His divinity. His love embraces even those who are now reproaching Him. "He overcame evil by goodness," says Saint Amphilochius. "He defended even those who put him to death. eager to gather them into His net. He cancelled their offense and pleaded their ignorance. Made the sport of their drunken frenzy, He submitted without bitterness. He suffered their drunkenness and in His love for all men called even them to repentance. What more could He do?"

He would leave nothing undone. He would spare nothing to deliver us from the slavery of sin. Only when He has accomplished this will He surrender His life. When it was accomplished He cried out, "It is finished!" In that cry He let all men of all time know that He surrendered His life, not because death had power over Him, but because He had the power to lay down His life of His own accord. "He gave up His spirit," says Saint Augustine, "in humility with a bowed head. With uplifted head He will receive it again in the resurrection."

brought me this man as one who was perverting the people; and after examining him before you, behold, I did not find this man guilty of any of your charges against him; neither did Herod, for he sent him back to us. Behold, nothing deserving death has been done by him; I will therefore chastise him and release him."

Christ or Barabbas

MATTHEW 27:15-23

Now at the feast the governor was accustomed to release for the crowd any one prisoner whom they wanted. And they had then a notorious prisoner, called Barabbas. So when they had gathered, Pilate said to them, "Whom do you want me to release for you, Barabbas or Jesus who is called Christ?" for he knew that it was out of envy that they had delivered him up. Besides, while he was sitting on the judgment seat, his wife sent word to him, "Have nothing to do with that righteous man, for I have suffered much over him today in a dream." Now the chief priests and the elders persuaded the people to ask for Barabbas and destroy Jesus. The governor again said to them, "Which of the two do you want me to release for you?" And they said, "Barabbas." Pilate said to them, "Then what shall I do with Jesus who is called Christ?" They all said, "Let him be crucified." And he said, "Why, what evil has he done?" But they shouted all the more, "Let him be crucified."

Jesus is scourged and crowned with thorns

MATTHEW 27:26-30

Then he released for them Barabbas, and having scourged Jesus, delivered him to be crucified.

Then the soldiers of the governor took Jesus into the praetorium, and they gathered the whole battalion before him. And they stripped him and put a scarlet robe upon him, and plaiting a crown of thorns they put it on his head, and put a reed in his right hand. And kneeling before him they mocked him, saying, "Hail, King of the Jews!" And they spat upon him, and took the reed and struck him on the head.

Pilate's last resistance

MATTHEW 27:24-25

So when Pilate saw that he was gaining nothing, but rather that a riot was beginning, he took water

"I am innocent of this man's blood."

and washed his hands before the crowd, saying, "I am innocent of this man's blood; see to it yourselves." And all the people answered, "His blood be on us and on our children!"

JOHN 19:4-15

Pilate went out again, and said to them, "Behold, I am bringing him out to you, that you may know that I find no crime in him." So Jesus came out, wearing the crown of thorns and the purple robe. Pilate said to them, "Here is the man!" When the chief priests and the officers saw him, they cried out, "Crucify him, crucify him!" Pilate said to them, "Take him yourselves and crucify him, for I find no crime in him." The Jews answered him, "We have a law, and by that law he ought to die, because he has made himself the Son of God." When Pilate heard these words, he was the more afraid; he entered the praetorium again and said to Jesus, "Where are you from?" But Jesus gave no answer. Pilate therefore said to him, "You will not speak to me? Do you not know that I have power to release you, and power to crucify you?" Jesus answered him, "You would have no power over me unless it had been given you from above; therefore he who delivered me to you has the greater sin."

Upon this Pilate sought to release him, but the Jews cried out, "If you release this man, you are not Caesar's friend; every one who makes himself a king sets himself against Caesar." When Pilate heard these words, he brought Jesus out and sat down on the judgment seat at a place called The Pavement, and in Hebrew, Gabbatha. Now it was the day of Preparation for the Passover; it was about the sixth hour. He said to the Jews, "Here is your King!" They cried out, "Away with him, away with him, crucify him!" Pilate said to them, "Shall I crucify your King?" The chief priests answered, "We have no king but Caesar."

Jesus is condemned to be crucified

LUKE 23:24-25

So Pilate gave sentence that their demand should be granted. He released the man who had been thrown into prison for insurrection and murder, whom they asked for; but Jesus he delivered up to their will.

Jesus takes up His cross.

CRUCIFIXION AND DEATH OF CHRIST

The way of the cross

LUKE 23:26-32

And as they led him away, they seized one Simon of Cyrene, who was coming in from the country, and laid on him the cross, to carry it behind Jesus. And there followed him a great multitude of the people, and of women who bewailed and lamented him. But Jesus turning to them said, "Daughters of Jerusalem, do not weep for me, but weep for yourselves and for your children. For behold, the days are coming when they will say, 'Blessed are the barren, and the wombs that never bore, and the breasts that never gave suck!' Then they will begin to say to the mountains, 'Fall on us'; and to the hills, 'Cover us.' For if they do this when the wood is green, what will happen when it is dry?"

Two others also, who were criminals, were led away to be put to death with him.

Christ is crucified

MARK 15:22-24a,25

And they brought him to the place called Golgotha (which means the place of a skull). And they offered him wine mingled with myrrh; but he did not take it. And they crucified him. And it was the third hour, when they crucified him.

The two thieves

MARK 15:27-28

And with him they crucified two robbers, one on his right and one on his left. And the scripture was fulfilled which says, "He was reckoned with the transgressors".

The title on the cross

JOHN 19:19-22

Pilate also wrote a title and put it on the cross; it read, "Jesus of Nazareth, the King of the Jews." Many of the Jews read this title, for the place where Jesus was crucified was near the city; and it was written in Hebrew, in Latin, and in Greek. The chief priests of the Jews then said to Pilate, "Do not write, 'The King of the Jews,' but, 'This man said, I am King of the Jews.'" Pilate answered, "What I have written I have written."

This is an awesome moment. Shocked, nature stands still. Then, revolting at the hideous crime, nature is seized with fits of violence. "The powers were astonished," says Alexander of Alexandria, "the angels wondered. The elements trembled. The whole created universe was shaken. The earth quaked and its foundations rocked. The sun fled away and the light of day withdrew. They could not bear to look upon their crucified Lord. All creation in amazement cried out, 'What is this awful mystery?'" The astonishment, however, does not prevail long. Immediately it gives place to victory, the greatest victory: love conquers death. Saint Peter Chrysologus describes how death is vanquished:

> Death is now judged. Death which seizes guilty men, now meets its Judge head on. Death, which held dominion over its slaves, now rises up against its Master. Death, which was victorious over men, now encounters God. In this conflict the dominion of hell perishes and its laws are blotted out. The power of death is destroyed, and in punishment for its rashness in attempting to harm its Judge it must bring its victims back to life.... Man is fashioned anew, his life restored, and now everything holds together through forgiveness because the condemnation of death has been swallowed up by the Author of life.

Expressing the same sentiments, Saint Cyril of Jerusalem exclaims:

> Death was struck with dismay when it beheld a new Visitor descending into hell who was not bound by the fetters of that place.... Death fled and his flight betrayed his cowardice.... All the holy ones of old whom death had devoured were ransomed. In such a way it was fitting for the King who had been heralded to become the Redeemer of His noble heralds. Then all the holy souls cried out: "O death where is thy victory? O death, where is thy sting?"

It was right that the loving Savior of all mankind should release the souls of the just of the Old Testament. They had lived in hope of His coming and now He had come to make them sharers in His glory. This Saint John Damascene explains:

> Just as the Son of holiness rose for those upon the earth, so likewise He brings light to those who sit under the earth in darkness and in the shadow of death. Just as He brought the message of peace to those upon the earth, releasing prisoners, restoring sight to the blind and being the Author of everlasting life for those who believe in Him, so now He goes down to be the same deliverer for those who hoped for His coming.

By His descent into the limbo of the just, the Redeemer threw His mantle of love over all those who had waited for His deliverance. With the same loving mercy He provided for the men and women of countless ages to come. At the moment that His spirit went forth to deliver the holy souls of the Old Law, His Body became the fountain of redemption for all men of the New Law. The soldier pierced His side with a lance, and at that moment the Church of the living was born. The parallel is striking. "Just as Adam was a figure of Christ," says Tertullian, "Adam's sleep foreshadowed the death of Christ. As Christ slept a mortal slumber,

The first word: forgiveness

LUKE 23:34a

And Jesus said, "Father, forgive them; for they know not what they do."

Christ's garments are divided

JOHN 19:23-24

When the soldiers had crucified Jesus they took his garments and made four parts, one for each soldier. But his tunic was without seam, woven from top to bottom; so they said to one another, "Let us not tear it, but cast lots for it to see whose it shall be." This was to fulfil the scripture.

"They parted my garments among them,
and for my clothing they cast lots."

The insults of the Jews and soldiers

MATTHEW 27:39-43

And those who passed by derided him, wagging their heads and saying, "You who would destroy the temple and build it in three days, save yourself! If you are the Son of God, come down from the cross." So also the chief priests, with the scribes and elders, mocked him, saying, "He saved others; he cannot save himself. He is the King of Israel; let him come down now from the cross, and we will believe in him. He trusts in God; let God deliver him now, if he desires him; for he said, 'I am the Son of God.'"

The second word: a promise of paradise

LUKE 23:39-43

One of the criminals who were hanged railed at him, saying, "Are you not the Christ? Save yourself and us!" But the other rebuked him, saying, "Do you not fear God, since you are under the same sentence of condemnation? And we indeed justly; for we are receiving the due reward of our deeds; but this man has done nothing wrong." And he said, "Jesus, remember me when you come in your kingly power." And he said to him, "Truly, I say to you, today you will be with me in Paradise."

The third word: Jesus bequeathes His mother

JOHN 19:25-27

So the soldiers did this; but standing by the cross of Jesus were his mother, and his mother's sister, Mary the wife of Clopas, and Mary Magdalene.

the wound was inflicted in His side. In the same manner as Eve was formed, the Church — true mother of the living — was formed from Christ's side." Rufinus continues the parallel in these words:

> If you ask why He is said to have shed water and blood from His side and not rather from some other part of His body, my answer is that His side with its rib mystically signifies a woman. The source of sin and death, you know, came from the first woman, who was the rib of the first Adam. Thus the source of redemption and life comes to us from the rib of the second Adam.

Saint Augustine continues the same comparison: "Without a doubt, the blood and water which poured forth from His side, when pierced by the lance, represent the sacrament by which the Church was formed, just as Eve was formed from the side of the sleeping Adam."

Over and above every other consideration, the cross of Christ stands out this day. That very same cross stands out every day in a Christian's life. Our lives as Christians are intimately woven around the cross. We cannot escape it. It is a part of our thinking, a part of our being. It is, first of all, a reminder of the Savior's infinite love; it is also a promise of our salvation and a pledge of our future glory. No wonder, then, that we should make the cross the symbol of our faith. With it we live; we have value. Without it we die, we are nothing. It is good for us, then, this day above all days, to meditate upon the cross of Christ.

At the very dawn of creation the cross was foreshadowed by the tree of good and evil. Just as that tree in paradise was the battleground between preternatural life and natural death, so the tree on Calvary was the battleground between supernatural life and eternal death. "Since death was by a tree," Saint John Damascene says, "it was fitting that life and resurrection should also be bestowed by a tree." Saint Irenaeus, relating the tree of paradise and the tree of the cross more closely, says:

> The disobedience caused by one tree was blotted out by the obedience of the other tree. Obedience to God was fulfilled when the Son of Man was nailed to the tree, destroying the knowledge of evil and conferring the knowledge of good. For evil is disobedience to God and goodness is obedience to God.... By hanging on the tree He obeyed even unto death and thus blotted out the old disobedience caused by the first tree.

If the cross of our Savior recalls the tree of paradise, it equally foretells all the graces that will come to man through the Church until the end of time. For both reasons the cross is to be considered much more a symbol of victory than an instrument of shame. This consideration prompted Saint Leo the Great to exclaim:

> O wondrous power of the cross! O unspeakable glory of the passion which became the Lord's tribunal, the world's judgment, and the power of the Crucified! From Your cross You draw all things to Yourself, O Lord! When You stretched out Your hands to an unbelieving people that mocked You, the whole world was finally brought to confess Your

When Jesus saw his mother, and the disciple whom he loved standing near, he said to his mother, "Woman, behold your son!" Then he said to the disciple, "Behold your mother!" And from that hour the disciple took her to his own home.

The fourth word: a plea for divine assistance

MARK 15:33-35

And when the sixth hour had come, there was darkness over the whole land until the ninth hour. And at the ninth hour, Jesus cried with a loud voice, "E'lo-i, E'lo-i, la'ma sabach-tha'ni?" which means, "My God, my God, why hast thou forsaken me?" And some of the bystanders hearing it said, "Behold, he is calling Elijah."

The fifth word: a cry of thirst

JOHN 19:28-29

After this Jesus, knowing that all was now finished, said (to fulfil the scripture), "I thirst." A bowl full of vinegar stood there; so they put a sponge full of the vinegar on hyssop and held it to his mouth.

The sixth word: consummation

JOHN 19:30a

When Jesus had received the vinegar, he said, "It is finished".

The seventh word: abandonment to God

LUKE 23:46

Then Jesus, crying with a loud voice, said, "Father, into thy hands I commit my spirit!" And having said this he breathed his last.

The death of Christ

MATTHEW 27:50

And Jesus cried again with a loud voice and yielded up his spirit.

Miracles that accompanied the death of Christ

MATTHEW 27:51-56

And behold, the curtain of the temple was torn in two, from top to bottom; and the earth shook, and the rocks were split; the tombs also were opened, and many bodies of the saints who had fallen asleep were raised, and coming out of the tombs after his resurrection they went into the holy city and appeared to many. When the centurion and those who were with him, keeping watch over Jesus,

majesty. When all the elements combined to pronounce judgment upon the crimes of the Jews, when the lights of heaven were extinguished and the day turned into night — You drew all things to Yourself, Lord.... In this way type gave way to truth, prophecy to revelation, the ancient law to the gospel. You drew all things to Yourself, Lord, so that what previously was performed in the one temple of the Jews in mystic signs is now celebrated everywhere by holy men in every country in revealing rites.... Your cross is the font of all blessings, the source of all graces, and through it the believers receive strength in return for weakness, glory in return for shame, life in return for death.

Saint Methodius is even more explicit in hailing the cross as the sign of victory: "The cross is the confirmation of victory, the way by which God descended to man, the trophy against the spirits of the world, the repulsion of death, the foundation of the ascent to veritable brilliance." Rufinus sees the cross as a victory over three kingdoms at one and the same time. "Consequently, a form of death was devised which symbolized this subjection. He was raised aloft in the air, thereby conquering the powers of the air and gaining a victory over the heavenly rulers. His outstretched hands He held out all day long to the people who were on earth, rebuking unbelievers and welcoming believers. And He subjugated the underworld through that portion of the cross that was buried in the earth."

Holy Mother Church emphasizes the glory of the cross in her liturgy today. She holds it high as the standard of salvation, the symbol of Christ's eternal victory. Like her divine Master, she can see in the cross only a claim to glory. "Every deed of Christ," says Saint Cyril of Jerusalem, "is a boast for the Catholic Church, but her greatest boast is the cross." For this reason Mother Church today asks her children to venerate the cross in a special way. She beseeches them to come forth and kiss the feet of the image of the Savior hanging on the cross. She urges them not to forget for a moment the cross and its values for the salvation of their souls. Little wonder, then, that the cross should be the sign Mother Church employs in all her sacred rites, for as Saint Augustine says:

> What other sign is *the* sign of Christ but the cross of Christ? Only through this sign are rites duly performed when it is applied on the brows of the believing, or over the water out of which they are reborn, or to the oil by which they are anointed with the chrism, or during the Sacrifice in which they are fed. Now who can say that no good is accomplished by what evil men do? We are signed with the cross of Christ (which evil men fashioned) in the celebration of His sacraments and thus we receive every good.

We can neither forget nor escape the cross. We see it on our buildings; we wear it on a chain around the neck; we engrave it on the covers of our books. But even if none of these signs were used, we could not escape the image of the cross. If evil men were some day to try to erase every man-made image of the cross, nature herself would preserve the sacred image of our salvation. This Saint Methodius explains when he says:

saw the earthquake and what took place, they were
filled with awe, and said, "Truly this was a son
of God!"

There were also many women there, looking from
afar, who had followed Jesus from Galilee, minister-
ing to him; among whom were Mary Magdalene,
and Mary the mother of James and Joseph, and the
mother of the sons of Zebedee.

The pierced heart

JOHN 19:31-37

Since it was the day of Preparation, in order to
prevent the bodies from remaining on the cross on
the sabbath (for that sabbath was a high day), the
Jews asked Pilate that their legs might be broken,
and that they might be taken away. So the soldiers
came and broke the legs of the first, and of the
other who had been crucified with him; but when
they came to Jesus and saw that he was already
dead, they did not break his legs. But one of the
soldiers pierced his side with a spear, and at once
there came out blood and water. He who saw it
has borne witness — his testimony is true, and he
knows that he tells the truth — that you also may
believe. For these things took place that the scripture might be fulfilled, "Not a bone of him shall be
broken." And again another scripture says, "They
shall look on him whom they have pierced."

The burial of Christ

JOHN 19:38-42

After this Joseph of Arimathea, who was a disciple of Jesus, but secretly, for fear of the Jews,
asked Pilate that he might take away the body of
Jesus, and Pilate gave him leave. So he came and
took away his body. Nicodemus also, who had at
first come to him by night, came bringing a mixture
of myrrh and aloes, about a hundred pounds' weight.
They took the body of Jesus, and bound it in linen
cloths with the spices, as is the burial custom of
the Jews. Now in the place where he was crucified
there was a garden, and in the garden a new tomb
where no one had ever been laid. So because of
the Jewish day of Preparation, as the tomb was
close at hand, they laid Jesus there.

Every creature has been marked with this sign for the sake of his own freedom. The birds which fly on high form the image of the cross by the expansion of their wings. Man, too, with his hands outstretched, represents the same sign of the cross. When the Lord fashioned man in this way at the beginning of time, He made his body form the sign of the cross to teach him that he would be for all time consecrated to God, freed from all discord and lack of harmony.

Such considerations on the cross of Christ should prompt us to make the sign of the cross reverently and frequently. It is our public confession of faith in our Savior. It is the weapon we use when the devil tempts us or the world tries to allure us. It is a reminder of our dignity and the price that was paid for our salvation. Saint Cyril of Jerusalem admonishes us:

Let us not be ashamed to confess the Crucified. Be the cross our sign made with boldness by our fingers on our brow and on everything: over the bread we eat, the cup we drink, in our coming and going, when we lie down and when we awake, when we are on a journey or remain at home. The cross has no price, for the sake of the poor. The cross demands no effort, for the sake of the sick. It is the sign of the faithful and the horror of the devils, for when they see the cross they are reminded of the Crucified and flee from us.

Death and life, triumph and tragedy, sorrow and joy, defeat and victory: these are the paradoxes of Good Friday. All center around the cross of Christ. Our lives, too, must center around the cross of Christ. "We should glory in the cross of our Lord Jesus Christ, in whom is our salvation, life, and resurrection; by whom we are saved and delivered."

The Sabbath rest

LUKE 23:56b

On the sabbath they rested according to the commandment.

The watch at the sepulchre

MATTHEW 27:62-66

Next day, that is, after the day of Preparation, the chief priests and the Pharisees gathered before Pilate and said, "Sir, we remember how that impostor said, while he was still alive, 'After three days I will rise again.' Therefore order the sepulchre to be made secure until the third day, lest his disciples go and steal him away, and tell the people, 'He has risen from the dead,' and the last fraud will be worse than the first." Pilate said to them, "You have a guard of soldiers; go, make it as secure as you can." So they went and made the sepulchre secure by sealing the stone and setting a guard.

THE VIGIL OF HOLY EASTER

You walk out into the night. The air is fresh and crisp, full of expectancy. You drive to church with your family. You greet your neighbors as you enter the church. Although no one says it, you know you are going to participate in one of the great events of the year. This is the night of the great vigil, the Easter vigil. Saint Augustine tells us why it is so great:

> How eagerly we should keep watch during this vigil, the mother of all the sacred vigils.... On this sacred night the whole world keeps vigil, both the world that hates Christ as well as the world that has been restored by Him. The latter, now delivered from sin, watches because it wants to praise its deliverer; the former, now condemned, watches for an opportunity to blaspheme its judge. The latter keeps watch with a fervent and loving mind; the former with weeping and gnashing of teeth. Love inspires the latter; hate moves the former. Thus, unwittingly, even our enemy teaches us how we should keep watch tonight, for he who envies us keeps watch in order to ensnare us... Let us, then, watch and pray so that both externally and internally we may fittingly celebrate this vigil.

Why do we assemble in our parish church with friends and neighbors tonight? "We prolong our singing tonight," St. Augustine says, "because He in whose honor we sing will grant us to reign with Him in eternal life."

It seems long ago that we heard the dreadful cry, "It is consummated." Our Savior has rested in the tomb. He has, to be sure, suffered the penalty of death. But for Him this was not so much a penalty as a prologue. Now we gather together to share in the glory of His resurrection.

Again the scenes have changed swiftly. Penitence and sorrow are things of the past. Holy hope and confidence fill our hearts and souls tonight. We come together in joy to begin our celebration. "This celebration," Saint Augustine reminds us, "has made this night the most important of all nights in the whole world." This is our great moment precisely because it was, and continues to be, the Savior's greatest moment. We watch and wait to

THE RISEN CHRIST

THE DAY OF THE RESURRECTION

The women at the grave

MARK 16:1-4

And when the sabbath was past, Mary Magdalene, and Mary the mother of James, and Salome, bought spices, so that they might go and anoint him. And very early on the first day of the week they went to the tomb when the sun had risen. And they were saying to one another, "Who will roll away the stone for us from the door of the tomb?" And looking up, they saw that the stone was rolled back; for it was very large.

Mary Magdalene

JOHN 20:2

So she ran, and went to Simon Peter and the other disciple, the one whom Jesus loved, and said to them, "They have taken the Lord out of the tomb, and we do not know where they have laid him."

Angels appear to the holy women

LUKE 24:3-8

But when they went in they did not find the body. While they were perplexed about this, behold, two men stood by them in dazzling apparel; and as they were frightened and bowed their faces to the ground, the men said to them, "Why do you seek the living among the dead? Remember how he told you, while he was still in Galilee, that the Son of man must be delivered into the hands of sinful men, and be

see the Man of Sorrows transformed into the Victor who comes to make us
sharers in His victory.   Saint Peter Chrysologus explains the meaning of this
mystery for us:

> You have seen that He was buried so that no one could say His death
> was only imaginary.... Christ devoted the three days of His burial to
> the three abodes He was going to deliver, namely, the region beneath the
> earth, the earth, and heaven.   He was going to restore all the things in
> heaven, repair the things on earth, and redeem those beneath the earth
> by this period of His three days' rest.   In this way He opened the grace
> of the Blessed Trinity to all men for their salvation.

The contrast is striking.   It seems almost impossible that such transforma-
tion and transfiguration could happen in so short a time.   If it seems
shocking, it is so only to those who have no hope.   For us Christians, however,
this is the great feast of hope.   It embodies the conflict between light and
darkness, between the glory of heaven and the damnation of hell.   With this
thought in mind Saint Amphilochius cries out:

> Death has seized our Lord Jesus Christ but shall not keep its hold on life.
> It swallowed Him not knowing Him and, in returning Him to life, restores
> all of us to life.   Of His own free will He is now held by death.   Tomorrow
> He shall rise again and hell shall be emptied.   Yesterday, on the cross, He
> darkened the sun's light so that in the middle of the day it appeared to
> be night.   Today death has lost its power and appears almost to have
> died itself.   Yesterday the earth mourned and in sadness clothed itself
> in a garment of darkness.   Today the people who walk in darkness have
> seen a great light.

The feast of light!   How the Church dwells on the image!   The paschal
candle, symbol of Christ, is lighted and carried into the church.   The great
paschal hymn, the *Exsultet,* is sung by the deacon in praise of the great
light that now shines in the house of the faithful.   The comparison is
evident: sin hides in the darkness of confusion; life delights in the brightness
of the great light.   Again we perceive the admirable exchange: we walk
from the darkness of death into the brightness of life because the Savior
has prepared the ground and given us sure footing.   The Venerable Bede
explains it in this way:

> From the beginning of earthly creation until now the course of time has
> been so divided that day preceded night.   This was so because man got lost
> in the confusing darkness of this world after he fell from paradise because
> of his sin.   But now day fittingly follows night, since through faith in
> the resurrection we are, through the mercy of Christ, brought back from
> the shadow of death and the darkness of sin into the light of life.

The riches of this night are here for all of us to make our own.   There is
little need for human words or pious exhortation.   The symbolism of every
action performed tonight should be obvious to all.   "God does not call us,"
explains Saint Hilary of Poitiers, "to the blessed life through arduous investi-
gations.   He does not tempt us with the studied arts of rhetoric.   The way
to eternity is plain and easy: believe only that Jesus rose from the dead
through His own power and confess that He is the Lord."   All great events,

crucified, and on the third day rise." And they
remembered his words,

The women inform the apostles

LUKE 24:9-11

and returning from the tomb they told all this to
the eleven and to all the rest. Now it was Mary
Magdalene and Jo-anna and Mary the mother of
James and the other women with them who told
this to the apostles; but these words seemed to them
an idle tale, and they did not believe them.

Peter and John

JOHN 20:3-10

Peter then came out with the other disciple, and
they went toward the tomb. They both ran, but
the other disciple outran Peter and reached the
tomb first; and stooping to look in, he saw the
linen cloths lying there, but he did not go in. Then
Simon Peter came, following him, and he went into
the tomb; he saw the linen cloths lying, and the
napkin, which had been on his head, not lying with
the linen cloths but rolled up in a place by itself.
Then the other disciple, who reached the tomb first,
also went in, and he saw and believed; for as yet
they did not know the scripture, that he must rise
from the dead. Then the disciples went back to
their homes.

The women find the tomb empty.

like all great mysteries, are simple. Tonight we need only to confess our belief in the simple fact of the resurrection. With this truth as a starting point, the whole meaning and purpose of our salvation is evident. The Venerable Bede spells out what this belief implies:

> We must believe that our bodies also shall be endowed with heavenly glory after their resurrection. They shall have power to do what they please and shall be free to go wherever they wish. . . . The children of the resurrection shall have no other food or drink than true life and salvation, joy, peace, and every good.

This is the holy hope of future joy that our faith now promises us. This is the assurance that each of us receives tonight because our Savior has prepared a place for us. He is the first-born of the new creation effected by His resurrection. We are His brothers and with Him sharers in a new life. This simple truth is brought home to us tonight with a renewed force and vigor. Our faith is strengthened, our hope renewed, our charity rekindled because we have come together tonight to return with the Christian community to the very foundation of our religion. Tonight, above all other times in the year, are the words of Saint Ambrose fulfilled in our lives:

> We have seen how serious an offense it is not to believe in the resurrection, for if we do not rise again, then Christ died in vain and — in fact — Christ Himself never rose again from the dead. For certainly, if He did not rise for us, He arose for no one, since He had no need to rise only for Himself. We know, however, that the universe rose again in Him, heaven rose again in Him, and the earth rose again in Him, for there shall now be a new heaven and a new earth.

Everything about the prayers and rites tonight is oriented to the sacrament of baptism, in which we received the three great virtues of Christian living. Christ dies — to rise with newness of life; in baptism we too die — to rise with newness of life. The new members of our parish community are brought forward to be baptized. We ourselves are asked by our father in Christ to renew our baptismal promises. Saint Leo the Great states succinctly the effect of baptism:

> Passing from the old state into a new life and casting off our earthly image in exchange for a supernatural identity is a sort of dying and rising again. Thus he who is received by Christ as well as he who actually receives Christ is not the same after he comes to the font as he was before. His body now becomes the flesh of the Crucified.

The sacred actions performed before us and for us tonight move swiftly. We pass quickly from the blessing of the baptismal water to the renewal of baptismal vows until we stand before the altar of the Lord to join in the great hymn of eucharistic praise. This is the Mass of the resurrection. We gather about the altar tonight, as the holy women gathered about the tomb. From them we should learn how we should act on this most sacred of all nights. Saint John Chrysostom draws these lessons from the behavior of the holy women:

> These holy women spent a great deal and exposed themselves to many dangers in order to care for Him whom they thought was dead. But we

Jesus appears to Mary Magdalene, then to the other women

JOHN 20:11-18

But Mary stood weeping outside the tomb, and as she wept she stooped to look into the tomb; and she saw two angels in white, sitting where the body of Jesus had lain, one at the head and one at the feet. They said to her, "Woman, why are you weeping?" She said to them, "Because they have taken away my Lord, and I do not know where they have laid him." Saying this, she turned round and saw Jesus standing, but she did not know that it was Jesus. Jesus said to her, "Woman, why are you weeping? Whom do you seek?" Supposing him to be the gardener, she said to him, "Sir, if you have carried him away, tell me where you have laid him, and I will take him away." Jesus said to her, "Mary." She turned and said to him in Hebrew, "Rab-boni!" (which means Teacher.) Jesus said to her, "Do not hold me, for I have not yet ascended to my Father and your Father, to my God and your God." Mary Magdalene went and said to the disciples, "I have seen the Lord"; and she told them that he had said these things to her.

The guards and the chief priests

MATTHEW 28:11-15

While they were going, behold, some of the guard went into the city and told the chief priests all that had taken place. And when they had assembled with the elders and taken counsel, they gave a sum of money to the soldiers and said, "Tell people, 'His disciples came by night and stole him away while we were asleep.' And if this comes to the governor's ears, we will satisfy him and keep you out of trouble." So they took the money and did as they were directed; and this story has been spread among the Jews to this day.

The disciples at Emmaus

LUKE 24:13-32

That very day two of them were going to a village named Emmaus, about seven miles from Jerusalem, and talking with each other about all these things that had happened. While they were talking and discussing together, Jesus himself drew near and went with them. But their eyes were kept from recognizing him. And he said to them, "What

neither feed Him when hungry nor clothe Him when naked, and when we see Him begging, we pass Him by.... It is not nearly such a great deed to feed Him when He appears to you in His own person as it is to serve the poor, the maimed, and the down-trodden for His sake.... In the latter case we show Him greater reverence, since by following His words and serving our fellow man we refresh Him in all things.

As the women approached the tomb, the earth quaked and they heard a mighty roar. "The earthquake," says Saint Hilary of Poitiers, "signified the power of the resurrection. Hell is now shaken with alarm because the sting of death is crushed and the dark places are filled with light through the rising of the Lord of hosts." Entering the tomb, the holy women see an angel sitting near the place where they had laid His sacred Body. The Venerable Bede sees a hidden meaning even in the very posture of the angel:

> Rightly did the angel stand who foretold the coming of the Lord into the world. The angel's stance showed that the Lord would come to wage war against the prince of this world. But the herald of the resurrection is sitting to show that the Lord, having overthrown the author of death, would now ascend to the throne of His Kingdom. He sat upon a stone rolled back from the entrance of the tomb to show that the Lord had thrown open the gates of hell by His own power.

This night encompasses all the paradoxes of Christian living. Rather, Christ the Conqueror embodies in His own person all the seeming contradictions of all who strive to lead good Christian lives. What happened on this night? Why were the tables turned? Saint John Chrysostom offers this answer:

> Those who previously seemed to have conquered were above all others put to shame, defeated and ruined. He who seemed to have been defeated on Good Friday now arises in brilliant and mighty conquest.... Thus it is for each of us. He who is dragged to martyrdom conquers by being bound, beaten, maimed and slain. Nowhere do we overcome by doing harm. Everywhere we triumph by enduring unjust punishment. This shows that true victory is from God.... Knowing these things, then, let us pursue the true victory which is gained by suffering unjustly and fleeing from all wrong-doing. In such a way we shall live this present life in all tranquility and at the same time receive all the good things of the future life through the grace and love of our Lord Jesus Christ.

His victory is ours; His glory is ours. He has lifted us up, drawing us to Himself; and in Him we have found our new life. So tonight we shout, "Alleluia!" We shall continue to sing our "alleluias," for our entire life as Christians should be one prolonged "alleluia." And if we ask what this strange word means, Saint Augustine tells us "it is a Hebrew word signifying 'praise God.'" By our "alleluias," then, we cry out ceaselessly, "praise God," and thus encourage all creation to join in our hymn of praise.

We leave the church and go back out into the cool spring air. The strains of "alleluias" ring in our ears. New Easter clothes are but an outward manifestation of the new life that has come to us through the resurrection of Christ. We greet our neighbors more warmly, now understanding better our oneness in Christ. Even the world looks better, brighter. We exchange

Jesus accompanies two disciples to Emmaus.

is this conversation which you are holding with each other as you walk?" And they stood still, looking sad. Then one of them, named Cleopas, answered him, "Are you the only visitor to Jerusalem who does not know the things that have happened there in these days?" And he said to them, "What things?" And they said to him, "Concerning Jesus of Nazareth, who was a prophet mighty in deed and word before God and all the people, and how our chief priests and rulers delivered him up to be condemned to death, and crucified him. But we had hoped that he was the one to redeem Israel. Yes, and besides all this, it is now the third day since this happened. Moreover, some women of our company amazed us. They were at the tomb early in the morning and did not find his body; and they came back saying that they had even seen a vision of angels, who said that he was alive. Some of

greetings with everyone; and no matter what words we use, they echo our "alleluias." We are dedicated anew, incorporated again, in the life of the risen Savior. We are commissioned by Him to offer with Him and in Him an everlasting "alleluia." We were made to praise God. This is our joy. This is our glory. This is our resurrection.

We slowly begin to make our way back home. As we depart, Saint Leo the Great gives us a final admonition:

> We must keep these thoughts in mind, dearly beloved, not only during this Easter festival but for the hallowing of our entire lives. We should consider these present religious exercises and all the delights that we have experienced during this short observance but a prelude to an entire life of goodness. If any fault creeps into your lives, destroy it immediately through sincere repentance. Since the curing of deep-rooted diseases is a slow and difficult process, apply remedies early, when the wounds are still fresh. Thus we shall continually rise from our faults and merit to share in the everlasting resurrection of our own glorified bodies in Christ Jesus our Lord, who lives and reigns with the Father and the Holy Spirit forever and ever. Amen.

EASTER SUNDAY

Joy and glory. We cry out "Alleluia," praising the Lord who is risen and with us, soon to return to heaven and then to be even more closely with us. "Alleluia," we shout, the Christian's song of joy and glory.

The "alleluia" is more than a word tacked on at the end of a prayer; it is even much more than an expression of our joy and glory on Easter morning and throughout the Easter season. "Alleluia" is a state of existence; it expresses what the Christian life truly is. St. Methodius extends the Church's invitation: "Sing a new hymn of conquest and a new song of peace to Christ who gained the victory. Come, everyone, and rejoice in the Lord!"

Easter candle and Easter water, Easter eggs and Easter bonnets all are expressions of the new life that has risen in our midst. The world rises from death to greet the Son of the resurrection. All men are restored; all men are reborn; all men are charged with the spark of glory from the glorious One who draws each of us into the joy of His resurrection. This is more than history, infinitely more than a pious remembrance. The resurrection continues to happen. Christ continues to be the unvanquished Victor. He continues to speak every Easter dawn of every Christian's life: "Have confidence; I have overcome the world."

Today holy Mother Church uses Saint Methodius's exhortation to his people long ago:

those who were with us went to the tomb, and
found it just as the women had said; but him they
did not see." And he said to them, "O foolish men,
and slow of heart to believe all that the prophets
have spoken! Was it not necessary that the Christ
should suffer these things and enter into his glory?"
And beginning with Moses and all the prophets, he
interpreted to them in all the scriptures the things
concerning himself.

So they drew near to the village to which they
were going. He appeared to be going further, but
they constrained him, saying, "Stay with us, for it
is toward evening and the day is now far spent."
So he went in to stay with them. When he was
at table with them, he took the bread and blessed,
and broke it, and gave it to them. And their eyes
were opened and they recognized him; and he van-
ished out of their sight. They said to each other,
"Did not our hearts burn within us while he talked
to us on the road, while he opened to us the scriptures?"

MARK 16:12

After this he appeared in another form to two
of them, as they were walking into the country.

Their report to the apostles in Jerusalem

LUKE 24:33-35

And they rose that same hour and returned to
Jerusalem; and they found the eleven gathered together and those who were with them; who said,
"The Lord has risen indeed, and has appeared to
Simon!" Then they told what had happened on the
road, and how he was known to them in the breaking of the bread.

Jesus appears to the apostles in the
absence of Thomas

LUKE 24:36-43

As they were saying this, Jesus himself stood
among them. But they were startled and frightened,
and supposed that they saw a spirit. And he said
to them, "Why are you troubled, and why do ques-
tionings rise in your hearts? See my hands and
my feet, that it is I myself; handle me, and see;
for a spirit has not flesh and bones as you see
that I have." And while they still disbelieved for
joy, and wondered, he said to them, "Have you
anything here to eat?" They gave him a piece of
broiled fish, and he took it and ate before them.

> Come, beloved, and let us with willing hearts and open minds listen to
> what the Lord our God shall say . . . He will speak to His people and
> His saints and to all who open their hearts to Him.   Today the trumpet
> blast of the prophets has aroused the world and has filled with joy and
> gladness the churches of God scattered among the nations.

This is Easter, the day of the Lord.   "Let us rejoice," the psalmist cries out,
"and be glad in it" (Ps. 117:24). Enraptured by the joy and glory of this
day, Saint Gregory Nazianzen exclaims, "O Pasch! Great and holy, purifier
of all the world!   O work of God, light and life, wisdom and power!   I rejoice in all your names!   O child of that great mind, His desire and His
image!"   Have we lost our capacity for wonderment?   Have we forgotten in
the dreariness of living the freshness of a child's joy?   Our sophistication
might have dulled us.   Our learning might have made us deaf to the sounds
of spiritual joy and have blinded us to the sights of Christian gladness.   If so,
we have made ourselves paupers by seeing only half of the canvas.   Forty
days we spent, devotedly and sometimes drudgingly, following the Savior
up to Calvary's summit.   But we cannot stop there.   Calvary is only the
beginning.   Christ suffered crucifixion as the condition of resurrection.   The
Man of sorrows of Good Friday is the King of glory for all times.   A Christian
must suffer; but suffering is only his passport to glory.   Joy is the essence of
Christianity.   Glory is the result of Christian living.   Joy and glory!   Alleluia!   This is the eternal fulfillment of Christian living, but this joy and glory
and alleluia of praising God begins on earth.

The Church teaches the same lesson in her liturgy.   Saint Augustine
explains that lesson when he says:

> These holy days which are celebrated after the resurrection of the Lord
> signify the life that is to come after our resurrection.   The forty days
> before Easter symbolized the life of suffering in this mortal life.   Now,
> however, these joyful days point to the future life when we are destined
> to reign with the Lord.   The life signified by the forty days before Easter
> we are living now.   The life symbolized by the fifty days after Easter is
> not yet possessed, but it is hoped for and loved all the while we are
> awaiting it.   That very desire is our way of praising God who promised
> us eternal life—and our praises are alleluias.

The accent must always be on joy and glory.   Our life is one of joyful
service to God and His people.   Our efforts are works of glory when they
are united to the glorious works of God.   The Eastern mind understands this
better than our departmentalized Western mind.   The earlier Christians, too,
gave witness to the resurrection by the glorious joy of their lives.   Their joy
was contagious, giving us an example of the spirit we must restore to our
muddled and confused world.   Saint Proclus gives testimony to the joy of
his people:

> Glorious is our paschal festival!   How splendid is this great assembly of
> the Christian people!   In this holy mystery are contained many things,
> both old and new.   The celebration — rather, the joyfulness — of this week
> is shared by such a multitude that not only man rejoices on earth but
> even the heavenly powers join us in the joyful celebration of Christ's
> resurrection.   The angels and the hosts of archangels make holiday, stand-

OTHER APPEARANCES
OF THE RISEN SAVIOR

Jesus again appears to the eleven in Jerusalem

MARK 16:14

Afterward he appeared to the eleven themselves as they sat at table; and he upbraided them for their unbelief and hardness of heart, because they had not believed those who saw him after he had risen.

JOHN 20:24-29

Now Thomas, one of the twelve, called the Twin, was not with them when Jesus came. So the other disciples told him, "We have seen the Lord." But he said to them, "Unless I see in his hands the print of the nails, and place my finger in the mark of the nails, and place my hand in his side, I will not believe."

Jesus appears to His apostles.

ing in attendance as they await the triumphant return from earth of Christ our Lord, the King of heaven. The multitude of the saints also rejoice, bearing witness to Christ who was born before the day star rose. The earth rejoices, for she has been washed by divine Blood. The sea rejoices, for it has been honored by His feet upon its waters. Above all else, let every soul rejoice! . . By His resurrection Christ fills our hearts with great joy this day. He makes us glad today because He has saved us through His passion, given us immortality through His death, healed our wounds and lifted us up by His resurrection!

"O Pasch! great and holy, purifier of all the world." Saint Gregory's words echo throughout the day, throughout the season, throughout the Christian life. Saint Leo the Great explains the word for us:

> Since you are celebrating the holy Pasch, you should know, brethren, what the Pasch is. It means the "crossing-over". . . . On this day the children of Israel crossed over from Egypt to the promised land and the Son of God crossed over from this world to His Father. There is no profit in celebrating the Pasch, then, unless you imitate the Lord whom you worship. That means you must cross over from Egypt (that is, the darkness of evil-doing) to the light of virtue. You must cross over from the love of this world to the love of your heavenly home.

Easter and resurrection, ascension and heaven; neither can be separated from the other. Passing from death-to sin to life-in-Christ is but the first step of the passage from earthly joy to eternal glory. Easter points heavenward, as surely as our new life in Christ is already the beginning of heaven on earth. The resurrection prepares us for our own ascension; we trace the footsteps of the glorious One. Examples from the story of the resurrection point our way to heaven.

The evangelists tell us that the women came to the tomb "very early in the morning." From this phrase the Venerable Bede draws this application:

> Mystically, this gives us the example of how, scattering the darkness of vices and turning our face to the light, we should be earnest in offering the Lord the odor of our good works and the sweetness of our prayer.

Speaking more directly so that none of his people could possibly miss the lesson, Saint Ambrose asks the question:

> What were these holy women seeking at the tomb, if not Jesus our Savior? If you wish to find Him, come as these women came when the sun is risen. Let no darkness of evil be in your hearts, for the desires of the flesh and evil deeds are darkness. Those whose hearts are filled with this kind of darkness cannot see the light and cannot understand Christ, for Christ is the light. Therefore, brothers, drive the darkness from you (that is, all sinful desires and evil deeds) and secure sweet spices (that is, earnest prayer). Then cry out with the psalmist, "Let my prayer be counted as incense before Thee."

At every great moment in Christ's life on earth, angels were present. An angel announced His coming and a host of angels proclaimed His glory the night of His birth. An angel strengthened Him in the lonely hour of His passion and an angel announced His resurrection. The holy women at

Eight days later, his disciples were again in the house, and Thomas was with them. The doors were shut, but Jesus came and stood among them, and said, "Peace be with you." Then he said to Thomas, "Put your finger here, and see my hands; and put out your hand, and place it in my side; do not be faithless, but believing." Thomas answered him, "My Lord and my God!" Jesus said to him "Have you believed because you have seen me? Blessed are those who have not seen and yet believe."

The appearance in Galilee; Jesus founds His apostolic Church

JOHN 21:1-23

After this Jesus revealed himself again to the disciples by the Sea of Tiberi-as; and he revealed himself in this way. Simon Peter, Thomas called the Twin, Nathana-el of Cana in Galilee, the sons of Zebedee, and two others of his disciples were together. Simon Peter said to them, "I am going fishing." They said to him, "We will go with you." They went out and into the boat; but that night they caught nothing.

Just as day was breaking, Jesus stood on the beach; yet the disciples did not know that it was Jesus. Jesus said to them, "Children, have you any fish?" They answered him, "No." He said to them, "Cast the net on the right side of the boat, and you will find some." So they cast it, and now they were not able to haul it in, for the quantity of fish. The disciple whom Jesus loved said to Peter, "It is the Lord!" When Simon Peter heard that it was the Lord, he put on his clothes, for he was stripped for work, and sprang into the sea. But the other disciples came in the boat, dragging the net full of fish, for they were not far from the land, but about a hundred yards off.

When they got out on land, they saw a charcoal fire there, with fish lying on it, and bread. Jesus said to them, "Bring some of the fish that you have just caught." So Simon Peter went aboard and hauled the net ashore, full of large fish, a hundred and fifty-three of them; and although there were so many, the net was not torn. Jesus said to them, "Come and have breakfast." Now none of the disciples dared ask him, "Who are you?" They knew the tomb, says Saint Severianus, "see a young man in order to understand the age of our resurrection, for resurrection knows no old age." Saint Jerome comments on the white garment worn by the angel:

> He appeared clothed with a white robe because he has announced the joys of our great feast. The shining whiteness of the garment proclaims the splendor of our festival. The enemy has been put to flight and the kingdom is restored. The shining white garment expresses great joy; the King of peace was sought and found and shall now never be forsaken.

Angels also appeared at the ascension. "And while they were gazing into heaven as He went," says the sacred writer, "behold, two men stood by them in white robes." The Fathers of the Church were fascinated by the white garments of the angels. Saint Gregory the Great says the white garments symbolize "a festive state of mind"; observing that the angels of the nativity had no white garments as did the angels of the resurrection, he goes on to explain:

> . . . there was great rejoicing among the angels when the Lord entered heaven. At His birth divinity seemed to have been humiliated. At His ascension humanity was exalted. White garments are more fitting for exaltation than humiliation.

For the early Church, moreover, the white garments had a deeper meaning than they have for us today. The early Christians saw this as the season of rejoicing for the growth of the Mystical Body since the catechumens had been baptized and now wore their white garments as a sign of their joy in sharing Christ's glory. Although we no longer wear the white robes of the neophytes, we too have renewed our baptismal promises on Holy Saturday night. Accordingly our souls are clothed with the mystical white garments of baptismal innocence and Christian joy. The words, then, that Saint Augustine directed to the neophytes of Hippo long ago apply with equal force to all of us today:

> Listen to me, you who have been baptized and reborn in the Blood of Christ . . . I beg you not to imitate your former companions so that the holy grace of Him who refused to descend from the cross but willed to rise again from the tomb may be in you always! Turning to the Lord our God, the almighty Father, let us give thanks from the bottom of our hearts and ask Him by His grace to drive evil from our thoughts and deeds, increase our faith, direct our thoughts, grant us His holy inspirations, and lead us to everlasting joy.

How much more deeply the neophytes of the early Church understood the likeness, or image, of Christ implanted in the soul of the Christian! They had a better grasp of the totality of redemption than we. They understood the role of the resurrection in mankind's salvation. Expressing this thought, Saint Augustine says:

> Christ is our salvation. He is our salvation when He was wounded for us, fastened with nails to the wood, taken down from the wood and laid in the sepulchre. But He also rose from the sepulchre; though His

it was the Lord. Jesus came and took the bread and gave it to them, and so with the fish. This was now the third time that Jesus was revealed to the disciples after he was raised from the dead.

When they had finished breakfast, Jesus said to Simon Peter, "Simon, son of John, do you love me more than these?" He said to him, "Yes, Lord; you know that I love you." He said to him, "Feed my lambs." A second time he said to him, "Simon, son of John, do you love me?" He said to him, "Yes, Lord; you know that I love you." He said to him, "Tend my sheep." He said to him the third time, "Simon, son of John, do you love me?" Peter was grieved because he said to him the third time, "Do you love me?" And he said to him, "Lord, you know everything; you know that I love you." Jesus said to him, "Feed my sheep. Truly, truly, I say to you, when you were young, you girded yourself and walked where you would; but when you are old, you will stretch out your hands, and another will gird you and carry you where you do not wish to go." (This he said to show by what death he was to glorify God.) And after this he said to him, "Follow me."

Peter turned and saw following them the disciple whom Jesus loved, who had lain close to his breast at the supper and had said, "Lord, who is it that is going to betray you?" When Peter saw him, he said to Jesus, "Lord, what about this man?" Jesus said to him, "If it is my will that he remain until I come, what is that to you? Follow me!" The saying spread abroad among the brethren that this disciple was not to die; yet Jesus did not say to him that he was not to die, but "If it is my will that he remain until I come, what is that to you?"

Commission of the apostles

MATTHEW 28:16-20

Now the eleven disciples went to Galilee, to the mountain to which Jesus had directed them. And when they saw him they worshiped him; but some doubted. And Jesus came and said to them, "All authority in heaven and on earth has been given to me. Go therefore and make disciples of all nations, baptizing them in the name of the Father and of the Son and of the Holy Spirit, teaching them to observe all that I have commanded you; and lo, I am with you always, to the close of the age."

wounds were healed, the scars remained. He felt this to be necessary for His disciples for by the scars He kept He is able to heal the wounds of their souls.

This, then, is the principal theme of the days of Easter: we rejoice because our glory is assured, not through our own merits but through the victory of Christ our Head. He has drawn us to Himself, caught us up in the infinity of His glory, and in a way made us sharers in His own divinity. Surely, then, we have every reason for rejoicing. We would not, in fact, be true to our Christian vocation if we did not rejoice. Saint John Chrysostom exhorts us:

> Let us celebrate this greatest and most shining feast in which the Lord has risen from the dead. Let us celebrate it with joyful devotion. The Lord has risen! He has lifted up the whole world with Him. The Lord has risen! He has shattered the chains of death.

Our joy reflects the joy of the Savior. We are born again in the likeness of His image, and this image is the shining brilliance of divinity. "Let us become like Christ," says Saint Augustine, "since Christ became like us. Let us become gods because of Him, since on account of us He became man."

Christian joy demands faith as much as future glory supposes hope. A time of joy, Easter is likewise a season of faith. The apostles themselves give us an example of the faith that should mark the Christian. Saint Ignatius of Antioch expresses the thought in these words:

> For my part, I know that even after His resurrection He was in the flesh and I believe this to be true. When He came to those who were with Peter, He said to them: "Handle Me, and see; for a spirit has not flesh and bones as you see that I have." As soon as they touched Him and felt His flesh and pulse, they believed. For this reason they later despised death and even showed themselves superior to death.

Holy hope, too, is assured by Christ's resurrection. The resurrection is the beginning of Christ's triumphant return to His heavenly Father. Because we are conformed to the likeness of His resurrection, we too are beginning our glorious return to the land of our spiritual birth. Thus Saint Augustine says:

> He rose again to give us hope that what dies will also rise again, lest death should cause us to despair and deceive us into thinking that our whole life has ended. As a matter of fact, we were anxious about our soul; by His resurrection He has now given us assurance about our body.... He came down from heaven to heal you; He returns to heaven to lift you up.

In another sermon the bishop of Hippo confirms our faith by stressing the unity of the Mystical Body of Christ: "He is the Head of the Church and the Church is His Body; the whole Christ is both the Head and the

The last instructions of Jesus

LUKE 24:44-49

Then he said to them, "These are my words which I spoke to you, while I was still with you, that everything written about me in the law of Moses and the prophets and the psalms must be fulfilled." Then he opened their minds to understand the scriptures, and said to them, "Thus it is written, that the Christ should suffer and on the third day rise from the dead, and that repentance and forgiveness of sins should be preached in his name to all nations, beginning from Jerusalem. You are witnesses of these things. And behold, I send the promise of my Father upon you; but stay in the city, until you are clothed with power from on high.

Jesus ascends into heaven

LUKE 24:50-53

Then he led them out as far as Bethany, and lifting up his hands he blessed them. While he blessed them, he parted from them. And they returned to Jerusalem with great joy, and were continually in the temple blessing God.

(ACTS 1:9-12)

And when he had said this, as they were looking on, he was lifted up, and a cloud took him out of their sight. And while they were gazing into heaven as he went, behold, two men stood by them in white robes, and said, "Men of Galilee, why do you stand looking into heaven? This Jesus, who was taken up from you into heaven, will come in the same way as you saw him go into heaven."
Then they returned to Jerusalem from the mount called Olivet, which is near Jerusalem, a sabbath day's journey away.

Body. He has already risen from the dead. Our Head, therefore, is in heaven." Then, boldly, Augustine concludes: "Where the Head is, there are the rest of the members. Let us not despair, for we shall follow our Head."

Follow our Head: these are words of faith and hope. No Christian doubts them; all Christians hope for their fulfillment. Saint Augustine continues:

> He has risen and ascended into heaven. There He must be followed. Heaven was far away from us before our Head had gone there. Now why should we despair if we are members of that Head? Who would be unwilling to follow Christ where there is supreme happiness, supreme peace and everlasting security?

Faith, Saint Paul tells us, is "the assurance of things to be hoped for, the conviction of things not seen" (Heb. 11:1). The resurrection caused consternation; the ascension turned bewilderment into confirmation of the fact that Christ lives; Christ reigns, and "of His kingdom there will be no end" (Lk. 1:33). Trying to probe the feelings of the apostles during these forty days of Easter, Saint Leo the Great explains:

> The blessed apostles, who had been encouraged by many miracles and instructed by many discourses, were still terrified by the cruelty of the Lord's passion. Only with great hesitation did they accept the reality of His resurrection. The Lord's ascension, however, gave them a new lease on life, turning fear into joy. They now directed their attention to His divinity, seeing Him enthroned at the Father's right hand. His bodily presence no longer prevented them from contemplating the Lord. He descended to earth yet did not leave the Father; now, ascending to heaven, He has not left His disciples.

Christian faith is strengthened rather than weakened by Christ's triumphant return to His Father's house. Saint Augustine puts these words into the Savior's mouth: "You do not wish to let Me go, for every man is reluctant to part with his friend.... But it is better for you that you no longer see Me in the flesh because then you will be able to contemplate My divinity. Externally I am leaving you; internally I shall fill you with Myself."

As it was with the apostles at the dawn of Christianity, so it is with us today. All that Christ did, He did for all men. As He conformed the apostles to the image of His resurrection, so today He incorporates us into that same likeness. As He strengthened the apostles' faith through the overpowering majesty of His divinity, so today He strengthens our faith. "He ascended into heaven," writes Saint Peter Chrysologus, "not to take Himself back into heaven (for He always remained there), but rather to lead there all of us whom He freed and snatch us from the powers of hell. Understand, then, that God has raised us up, planting our feet firmly in heaven and removing us from the slippery roads of the earth on which we are liable to fall." Although faith employs material signs and symbols, the more we detach ourselves from materiality, the stronger our faith

Christ, our Redeemer, has vanquished death.

becomes. No one understands this better than Christ Himself. Before His resurrection He was the man of the people, Jesus, the son of the carpenter of Nazareth. After His resurrection He withdraws from the mob. He is seen only by His intimate followers. Today He reigns as a hidden God, not seen by human eyes but known and loved by divine faith. "He became," says Saint Leo the Great, "more present to us in His divinity to the extent that His humanity became more removed from us."

Although we do not see His glorified Body, we live as members of His Mystical Body. The glorified Christ has no need of our service; the mystical Christ is always in need of love and service. During His life on earth Christ said to Nathanael, "You will see heaven opened, and the angels of God ascending and descending upon the Son of man" (Jn. 1:51). In a lengthy passage Saint Augustine makes an application for all of us:

> He would not say "ascending unto the Son of man" unless He were in heaven. Nor would He say "descending unto the Son of man" unless He were also on earth. At one and the same time He is both above and below; above in the unity of the Trinity, below in the needs of His people. He is above with the Father; He is below in us . . . . Fear Christ above; recognize Him below. Here He is poor, there He is rich. Rich, indeed, as the Son of man who has ascended into heaven and sits at the right hand of the Father. Yet He is still poor on earth in the poor, the hungry, the thirsty.

All that Christ did, He did for our instruction. Our present joy and future glory would be empty, indeed, if we did not profit from gladness in preparation for glory. Saint Gregory the Great exhorts us:

> Dearest brothers, we must follow Him in our hearts to where we believe He has ascended in His body. Let us turn away from earthly longings. Nothing here on earth can truly satisfy us. Reflect seriously on this fact. Although mild in countenance when He ascended, He shall be terrible when He returns. Now He commands with gentleness; then He shall exact with sternness. So let nobody waste this time of repentance which is granted us. Let nobody neglect to do all he can for his salvation.

The devout life leads to the glorious life. So faith tells us, hope promises us, charity assures us.

We repeat over and over, "This is the day which the Lord has made; let us rejoice and be glad in it" (Ps. 117:24). The day is great because it is already a foretaste of heaven. We rejoice and are glad because our King is enthroned, our Lord is glorified, our Head has imprinted the image of His glory on our souls. Little wonder, then, that Saint Jerome exclaims:

> A day of happiness now shines forth. It holds the primacy among all other days for the first light has shone upon it. On this day the Lord rises triumphant from the dead!